PARABLES FROM POACHERS

*Surviving 31 years
of poacher encounters
by the grace of God*

Joel D. Glover

Parables from Poachers
Surviving 31 years of poacher
encounters by the grace of God

Copyright 2018 Joel D. Glover

All Rights Reserved
No part of this book may be reproduced or transmitted in any form or by any means without written permission from the author.

ISBN: 978-0-9600469-0-4
Also available in Kindle and ePub formats

Book design and layout: Lighthouse24

Dedication

It was by the grace of God I survived over thirty years in wildlife law enforcement, and I thank and praise Him.

I thank my parents and sister and her family for their unwavering support. My mother and daddy provided all I needed to know how to make it in this life. Most importantly they took me to church, where I came to know the Lord at a young age. They could not have done anything more for me.

I thank the many officers whom I have worked with and who helped to shape me into the officer I was. There were many of them, and I thank them all.

The spouse and children of a law enforcement officer have a tough way to go. My family supported me 100 percent. I can't thank them enough. My wife is my soulmate—an incredible gift from God, and I thank Him for her every day. I love you my sweetheart.

God bless.

Contents

Preface 7
Introduction 11
Disclaimer 13

Blinded by the Light 15
Send You a Postcard! 25
It's Not What It Looks Like 29
Be Not Deceived 33
Fatal Variance 38
Decoy Christians 43
Get Him Out of My Sight 48
Sunday Come-to-Jesus Meeting 52
Second Chances 55
Bubba Plans to Kill 'Em 69
Will I Get My Gun Back? 74
Get That Light Outta My Face 80
I Don't Want to Go to Prison 84
We're Ready to Go! 93
Never Give Up 97
There Was My Hat 103
You Can't Straddle the Fence 107

Shots Fired in the Neighborhood	115
Joint Venture	121
Apples Don't Fall Far	127
Waiting for Daylight	136
We Play Hardball	139
It Was My Crossbow!	143
Thank Goodness It's the Game Warden	146
Don't Touch It!	149
Mistaken Identity	154
Corroborating Evidence	157
Best Friends?	163
Disposition	168
Compassion	171
By the Grace of God	176
Does It Make Any Difference?	181
Again?	185
Sliding and Shooting	191
And the Cuffs Wouldn't Fit!	197
Brigetta's Dibble	201
Not a Nice Person	205
Moment of Decision	214
Like Sausage through a Grinder	219
Start Praying	228
It's Who You Know	232
Divine Appointment	239

Preface

I LIVED A DOUBLE LIFE for thirty years. While employed with the Alabama Department of Conservation and Natural Resources, Wildlife and Freshwater Fisheries Division, Wildlife Section as a wildlife biologist, I also performed many of the law enforcement duties of a conservation enforcement officer (CEO). I quickly learned a large segment of the public considered anybody in a green state truck to be the game warden. I found it was often easier to accept that role than to explain the difference.

On my first day, Assistant Wildlife Section Chief Gary Moody informed me that while the fellow I was replacing had done an outstanding job as an area manager, he had alienated the conservation officers in the county. I was told it would be my job to rebuild the relationship with the officers. He instructed me to call game warden Earl Brown and to let him show me how to "do" law enforcement.

Although it was the county seat, Rockford had one gas station and one restaurant. Today it only has the gas station. The restaurant wasn't open every day. Most of their business was conducted on Friday evenings, when they served catfish. I decided to give it a try. When I arrived, I spotted a game and fish truck in the parking lot. I walked in and saw a game warden seated in a booth. I walked over and asked if he was Earl Brown. Never having been in law enforcement, I didn't realize someone inquiring as to who you are starts an officer's mind spinning to try to remember whether or not this is someone you've arrested or someone you should know or what their intention is. Today, after thousands of arrests, I know that all too well. Earl gave me a stern look and said, "I am." I extended my hand and introduced myself as the new area biologist. I informed him my assistant chief had instructed me to ask him to teach me how to do law enforcement. He looked as if I had told him he was going to have a root canal with no anesthesia. I told him I had a state radio and my number was 1741. Little did I know the wild ride I had climbed on.

Soon I met the other CEO in the county, Hershel Patterson. I would soon learn the two officers were pretty much polar opposites. Earl was very aggressive and often abrasive, while Hershel was much more laid back. I quickly learned they did not get along at all, and working with both of them was going to be a challenge. But I had been given my instructions, and I was going to make it work. Oh, to be young and naïve.

I had some success in getting the two officers to work together, and when we were working together, we accomplished a lot. Unlike most "biologists," I did not limit my enforcement work to the wildlife management area (WMA). The officers called me to work with them on whatever was going on wherever it was happening. Soon I was working on my own all over the county. This was very unusual, and many of the officers in surrounding counties didn't understand, and many didn't appreciate it. Several of them did not know how to take a "biologist" who wanted to do enforcement work. However, I became accepted by many of them, even some hardcore separatists. Therefore, I became somewhat of an anomaly. I did my best to glean the best traits from Earl and Hershel. I think it made me into a pretty good game warden, and I hope they would tell you that. Within a very few years, my number of cases was exceeding many officers across the state. It was during these times I witnessed many things that were hard to believe. I quickly realized people would do anything. Many of these stories will appear in this book. I assure you these stories are true and reflect my best recollections. Having just completed six years of college prior to getting hired, it was my nature to take really good notes. Those notes are the basis for many of these stories.

I give God praise for surviving my career. It is interesting how so many situations I found myself in mirrored the spiritual battles of life and reminded me of Bible passages. I have attempted to make this connection with this book. I hope you enjoy reading the stories. I thank God I survived them!

If you don't know Jesus as your Lord and Savior, I pray these parables from poachers will help you realize that is the most important decision you will ever make.

God bless.

Introduction

ON SEVERAL OCCASIONS, I have had the privilege to speak to men's groups and at wild game suppers. I normally always started the talk by sharing some of the tales of the crazy things that happened during my career. It soon became evident to me how the situations in these stories resembled the situations in our lives. Obviously, working in law enforcement was a continuous struggle between good and evil. This set the stage for the development of many tales and their application to life. I have chronicled many of these stories in this book.

I survived my career by the grace of a loving God—the same way you have survived to this point. Jesus said today is the day of salvation. Tomorrow isn't guaranteed. Jesus used parables to make people think for themselves; I hope something in the book speaks to you.

Disclaimer

IF YOU REMEMBER the television show *Dragnet*, you may recall the beginning with a disclaimer saying the stories you are about to see are true, but the names have been changed to protect the innocent. I must admit that always confused me. Why didn't they say the names have been changed to protect the guilty? Aren't the chances pretty good that if you make up a name it's going to belong to an innocent person? Now I understand if you depict some horrible crime and the guy's name is Robert Smith, then Robert Smith would rather you changed it. So, if you find a familiar name in this book, it may or may not be the person's real name. If it happens to be the name of the person seated next to you, and they get up and walk out when you start telling them about the story you are reading, it could be pure coincidence. You make up your own mind.

Blinded by the Light

(There They Are, Ronnie)

As the walking night hunter neared his location, I could hear the tension in the police officer's voice as he whispered over the radio, "I've got to get him." I knew it would be a stronger case if he allowed the man to pick up the deer. I also knew he wasn't used to facing armed outlaws in the dark. Against my instincts, I told him to go ahead and apprehend the subject and I would be there shortly.

The telephone ringer attached to my seat at the table was working well, as usual. During the Alabama deer season, it seemed as though every time I got the opportunity to sit down to a great meal prepared by my loving wife, the phone would ring with some type of hunting complaint. I answered the phone, and on the other end was one of the two Town of Rockford police officers.

Alan Rambo had begun his law enforcement career in the city of Montgomery; however, after several years, he had found the quiet little town of Rockford with its four hundred residents to be more to his liking. Alan lived about three miles east of town on Alabama Highway 22 in a little house that sat very near the road. He was not unlike most law enforcement officers I have encountered when it came to handling a wildlife violation. Many of these officers were well seasoned and had handled thousands of calls. They routinely answered dangerous calls I was glad I didn't have to deal with. However, in their view, calls with armed suspects illegally pursuing wildlife tended to rattle their cage. I quickly learned it was a matter of perspective. While approaching an armed subject was a regular occurrence for me, they weren't used to it. They, on the other hand, would charge right into situations I cautiously eased into it. It's all what you're used to.

As I listened on the phone, Alan excitedly related to me someone had just shot a deer in his yard. He reported the suspects were in a white Dodge dual-wheeled, extended-cab truck and were headed toward Rockford. I told him I was on the way and I would contact him by radio.

I strapped on my gun belt, told my wife I loved her, and headed out the door. Although the same is true for everyone, it was very evident to me, doing what I did, that there was no guarantee I'd be coming back through the door whenever I left home. Nevertheless, I dutifully jumped in my truck and turned it toward Rockford.

Rockford is a great little town in east central Alabama. The county seat of Coosa County, it lies forty-five miles north of Montgomery and about sixty-five miles south of Birmingham. Crime was normally at a minimum except for in the hunting season, when our business really picked up. At this time, Coosa County was the northern tip of Alabama's high whitetail deer population. Unfortunately, that made our county a hotspot for anyone wishing to hunt legally or, as it seemed was more often the case, illegally. Although there was plenty of open-permit hunting land and plenty of deer that could be taken during daylight hours, the deer standing along the side of the road often proved to be too great a temptation.

Although just a wide spot in the road, Rockford really was a type of oasis. After dark, it was the only place to purchase food, drink, or gas for twenty miles in any direction. Of course, after 10:00 p.m. you were out of luck, as there was not an open business anywhere in the county.

As I came over the hill and up to the only traffic light in town, a flashing red light, I looked across Highway 231 and into the parking lot of the discount food mart, or Majik Mart as it used to be named, and there sat a white Dodge dual-wheel, extended-cab pickup. Standing beside the truck was a fellow dressed in camo and looking like he was in a hurry to go somewhere. I turned south and quickly ducked behind the courthouse. I exited my truck and moved to a vantage point where I could observe the parking lot without being spotted. I had no doubt the truck was the right one. Alan had given an excellent detailed description, something that was so often lacking. I wish I had a dollar for every time a caller had given me a bad vehicle description. So many people would simply call and say "it was a truck" or "I think it was black." The almost universal description we received more than any other was a white Z71 pickup, and whatever the vehicle was, it always was reported to have a loud exhaust. Luckily, Alan had described this vehicle well.

Two individuals soon exited the store, and all three men climbed in the vehicle and headed toward the scene of the crime. I let them get out of sight and pulled out behind them. I radioed Alan and advised him they were coming back his way. I told him they would probably drop someone out at his house, and he needed to keep out of sight and allow them to get the deer. We were soon approaching his location, and he came over the radio and advised me they were stopping in front of his house. I told him I was not far behind them and to let them get the deer. He called back and said they had let a subject out of the truck and had driven off. I again reminded him to allow the subject to get the deer. I had pulled into a driveway and now had the landowner standing on the porch wanting to know who was out there. I quickly told him I was after some night hunters. With the night hunting problems we had, that was all it took for him to go back inside and turn off all his lights. While folks were happy to complain about night hunters, few wanted any part of trying to apprehend them.

I was not surprised someone had shot near Alan's house. It seemed every year the word would get out, in the outlaw hunting circles, about the sighting of a big buck or a deer with a drop tine or something unique. Once the word was "on the street," night hunters would regularly frequent the area, trying to get a glimpse of and hopefully a shot at the animal. I have caught several night hunters in the same place. Rumor was there was a white deer that had been seen in Alan's yard. Once that became known, the reports of the albino deer would run rampant. The truth is that albino deer are extremely rare. What had probably been observed was a deer with some white on it. While this wasn't an everyday occurrence, they were much more common than an albino. These deer are actually referred to as *piebald*. Their coloration is a result of the expression of a recessive gene. They normally don't survive for too long. But I digress.

The radio again crackled, and Alan reported the night hunter was scouring the yard with a light looking for the deer. I again advised him to hold tight. Seconds later he called back and said the subject was getting extremely close to his location. I again told him to hold tight and let the man get the deer. I could hear the uneasiness in his voice as he called back and stated the guy was right on top of him, and he was going to have to get him. Against my better judgment, I told him to go ahead and apprehend the subject, and I would go get the others.

I took off down the road and past his location to find the other two subjects, who I figured probably weren't far away. I had gone maybe a mile when I spotted their truck pulled off on the right side of the road. I eased up behind the truck and activated my blue lights. As I cautiously approached the vehicle, the driver asked what was going on, and I asked him the same question. The driver was a wiry guy dressed in camo and appeared to be about forty years old. He stated he had just pulled off the road to look at his map. I asked where he was trying to get to, and he told me he was camped down a side road and thought he might have run past it. I asked whose property he was camped on, and he replied he wasn't sure. This let me know he was playing it by ear, trying to come up with what he thought I would think were appropriate answers. I asked where he was hunting, and he replied he was here to hunt on the state management area located in the county. I asked when he planned to hunt there, and he replied this weekend. I could tell it rattled him when I informed him I was the wildlife manager on the area and it wasn't open for hunting this weekend. Seeing his story unraveling, he decided he would try getting a little belligerent and replied it really wasn't any of my business where he was going to hunt. With him on the ropes, I decided to turn up the heat.

I had noticed upon my arrival the passenger, a large guy, probably 250 pounds and with an apparent allergy to soap, was crammed into the fold-down seat behind the driver's seat. Therefore, I asked the driver if he always chauf-feured his passenger around in this manner when his front passenger seat was empty. If he was already on the ropes, now I had just landed a great right cross to the jaw. How do you answer that? It was rare that you would get that type of a gift handed to you. Obviously unable to come up with a good answer, the suspect became even more heated. Although I was enjoying having the upper hand, it was time to quit playing games. I informed the driver I was investigating a night-hunting incident in which he had taken part. He immediately stated he had no idea what I was talking about. I had anticipated that pitiful response and advised him he could deny it all he wanted, but I had a witness who had identified his truck, and, as a matter of fact, we had his front-seat passenger in custody now. He again claimed he didn't know what I was talking about; however, I detected a bit of a quiver in his voice. I told him he was under arrest for hunting at night, and whether he knew what I was talking about or not, he was going to jail. I had already called and asked the jail to send me a deputy to transport the two, and he soon arrived.

Now if you are a law-enforcement type or are just familiar with the parameters for making a warrantless arrest, you may be thinking I did not totally follow the correct procedure in this instance since I wasn't present when the illegal activity took place. Well, if you are thinking that, you are correct. However, during this time, night hunting of deer was rampant in Coosa County, and our district court judge and district attorney had given their blessing to this type of apprehension. The two subjects were loaded into the patrol car and transported to the Coosa County jail.

When I arrived at the jail, Alan had already arrived with the third subject. I immediately separated the three. In the tiny little jail, that meant one subject was with me in the 8'-by-8' booking/interrogation room, one was in the back room/deputy's office, and one would be held in the kitchen. I kid you not.

I entered the interrogation room and read the driver/vehicle owner his rights. I informed him his partner had been apprehended in the yard of the house near where they had shot, just as I had told him earlier, and the resident, a police officer, had seen the subject exit his truck. I let him think about that for a minute and then added his truck was subject to being confiscated. He immediately said, "You can't take my truck; I just paid $27,000 for it three weeks ago." I knew I now had his attention, and I assured him that upon his conviction, the truck was eligible to become part of our fleet. I let that hang in the air for a minute and then began questioning.

I started with the usual questions about "where had you been tonight" but soon got around to the incident at hand and asked him to tell me what had happened. Although he wanted to continue to proclaim his innocence, with the thought of losing his vehicle hanging in the balance, he evidently decided it was time to blame somebody else. He explained they had been coming down the road when the front-seat passenger had spotted some deer. Although he had told him not to shoot, he stuck his gun out the window and shot. I asked, "You told him not to shoot?" To which he responded, "I begged him not to shoot." I repeated, "You begged him not to shoot?" And he again replied, "I begged him not to shoot." As I considered his answers and jotted down some notes, the defendant asked me, "Who all has to know about this?" I responded that while it would be a matter of public record, I wouldn't have to tell anyone, but someone was going to have to get him out of jail. The man appeared visibly shaken by this. I escorted him back to the kitchen and retrieved the alleged shooter.

Ronnie was over six feet tall and slender. I advised him of his rights and asked him to tell me what had happened. Seeing how he was apprehended in the man's yard, he didn't try the "I didn't do anything" route. He stated they had been driving down the road when the driver spotted some deer and shouted, "There they are Ronnie! There they are Ronnie!" He added the driver had rolled down the electric window so he could get his gun out and shoot the deer. Noting a striking difference in the stories, I confirmed with him the driver had in effect instigated the night hunting. He repeated the driver had spotted the deer and told him to shoot them. He stated he always said if he ever got caught, he was going to give it up and sell his gun and light. I asked, "So you do this a lot?" He quickly replied, "No." I advised him he would not need to sell his gun and light. "I won't?" he excitedly asked, and I answered he would not have to do that since I felt certain those items would be confiscated and turned over to our department. He had a confused and sad look on his face as I escorted him back to the deputy's office and retrieved the back-seat passenger.

His story was that he was in the back seat and had no control over what had gone on. I informed him he had been on a joint venture and would be charged the same as the others. Those charges included hunting at night, hunting from a public road, hunting by aid of a vehicle, and hunting without a permit. I normally did not charge night hunters with hunting without a permit; however, seeing how the one fellow was out walking through the landowner's yard, I felt it was appropriate.

The three violators were given an opportunity to make a phone call, booked, and sent upstairs to a cell. Arresting three people on four charges each and placing them in jail results in a tremendous amount of paperwork. I was just finishing up when a lady arrived at the front door of the jail. She was buzzed in and came around the corner to the dispatcher area, where we sat talking about the case and finishing up paperwork. She rigidly stood at the door and disgustedly announced she was there to get Mr. Donovan. I told her he was upstairs in a cell, but we would retrieve him while the jailer explained the bonding process to her. The trustee went upstairs and got the violator. I was about to learn why the fellow had not wanted anyone to know about his predicament. As soon as he entered the room, he began apologizing to the woman. He had only uttered a few words when she gave him a crisp "shut up" command while holding up her index finger on her outstretched arm. He immediately shut up. To say she was upset with him would be a gross understatement. I later learned she was a captain in the air force, she had paid for the new truck, and she was in charge.

After she had made bond and they left, I was talking with Alan concerning the incident. I told him it was a very solid case; however, I wished the subject had found the deer before he apprehended him. We never found the deer. The officer said that as he had crouched in the yard watching, the subject had methodically searched the yard with the light strapped to his head. He explained the poacher had gotten so close he felt he had to apprehend him. Alan said when the guy turned away from him, he stood up and yelled, "Freeze, police!" Hearing this, the man spun around toward him, causing his head-mounted light to shine directly in Alan's eyes, blinding him. Alan stated that, temporarily blinded, he raised his pistol just above the light and shot, "and he hit the ground!" I have to think he hit the ground about as fast as my bottom jaw did when Alan told me he had shot over the fellow's head. He went on to say it was just instinct to fire over the guy's head when he was blinded by the light.

The defendants appeared in court, pled guilty, forfeited their guns and lights, and paid hefty fines. They never mentioned the warning shot, and I surely didn't.

You would think this would have taught these guys a valuable lesson; however, the shooter was caught night hunting again a few years later in an adjacent county. When the officer in that county contacted me to get an action summary of the case to use in court, I told him to ask ole Ronnie if anybody had shot over his head lately! Remarkably, as I was tweaking this story for publication, I heard an interesting news story from a nearby county. The report stated a United Parcel Service (UPS) driver was recovering from being shot in the arm by a bolt from a crossbow. A fellow practicing with his crossbow in his yard overshot his target, and the arrow hit the UPS driver as he drove past the house. I was not shocked to learn the crossbow shooter was Ronnie. You can't make this stuff up.

Let me assure you when you spend a lot of time working in the dark, you definitely need a dependable and bright flashlight. I have told many people I would rather leave home without my handgun than without my flashlight. While that may sound surprising, keep in mind I normally used the flashlight every night—the pistol, thankfully not so much.

When I say it was dark where I worked, I mean dark. Coosa County is 652 square miles in size and has a population of only 10,000 people. The Coosa wildlife management area was once listed on a stargazers' website as the darkest place in Alabama. I would hope we can all agree we are fortunate to have light. We take it for granted, yet we are lost without it. If you spend time in the dark, it's good to know there is light. Jesus said, "I am the Light of the world." He said those without light stumble in the darkness.

As we reflect on this story, I hope you realize the presence of light played a major role. The police officer was hit in the face with a beam of light, and it caused a reaction. The night hunter in the yard was hit in the face with the muzzle flash from a pistol being fired directly over his head, and it caused a reaction. So, what about you—what will be your reaction when you get hit in the face by the Light of the world? I heard a quote attributed to a source you probably didn't think I would use in this story: Mike Tyson. He reportedly said, "Everyone has a plan until they get hit in the face!" An encounter with the Light of the world, Jesus, demands a reaction. The response is up to you. You can stumble in the dark or come to the Light. I recommend you respond like the violator in this story—you fall to your knees. And while you are there, surrender to Jesus!

Send You A Postcard!

WHETHER WE REALIZE IT OR NOT, we all have a testimony. We live it out every day. Others hear it, see it, and evaluate it. The fellow in this story had a testimony that was obvious, comical, and tragic.

As CEOs in Alabama, we had full arrest powers, meaning we could arrest for any law violation committed in our presence. Of course, throughout my entire career, our department made it widely known they frowned heavily on us making any arrests other than for game and fish violations. However, when you worked the way we did, at the times we did, and in the places we did, it was inevitable we would run into numerous incidents where an arrest had to be made. Therefore, I made numerous arrests for driving under the influence (DUI), drug cases, theft of property, and others. These cases often were a pain. A custodial arrest in our rural county always meant you would spend at least a couple of hours taking the subject to jail and handling the appropriate paperwork, not to mention the follow-up time required in court and so forth. I never felt I could simply look the other way.

During the majority of my career, the town of Rockford, the county seat, had one police officer. The sheriff's office normally had one chief deputy, who was usually also the investigator, and three or four road deputies. With those few folks covering 652 square miles, anyone in need was glad to see any other officer, whether they were wearing blue, brown, or green.

At times, driving under the influence seemed to be nearly epidemic. With every DUI arrest, I couldn't help but feel I may have saved someone's life. During my career, I have observed several senseless fatalities due to alcohol abuse. Dealing with intoxicated individuals is always a grab bag in that you do not know what you may get. Some are ashamed and sorry for what they've done; some are upset over what the arrest will mean to their family, their job, and so on; and others are mean and belligerent. Interestingly, some are all of these things haphazardly alternating from one to another. As serious as the offense of driving under the influence is, at times the subjects could be quite humorous.

One night the county game warden and I were headed to the west part of Coosa County to work the night hunting of deer that was prevalent. As we drove west on Alabama Highway 22, we observed a vehicle being operated rather recklessly. The driver crossed the centerline on the two-lane road several times, and it seemed obvious to us they were impaired. We stopped the vehicle and found the driver was in fact highly intoxicated. Unfortunately, our patrol vehicle was a regular cab pickup. That meant our prisoner had to ride between us en route to the jail. Thankfully, it was a short trip. Otherwise, we all might have been drunk by the time we arrived. The smell of alcoholic beverage was so strong I was beginning to wonder whether the man had been drinking it or bathing in it!

While on the way to the county jail, I contacted the Rockford police chief and requested he come and administer the Intoxilyzer for us. The chief soon arrived, and we escorted the subject into the Intoxilyzer room. Before administering the breath test, the operator was required to read the suspect an implied consent paragraph concerning the test and the consequences if the test was refused. With the subject seated beside the machine and a fresh mouthpiece in place, the chief began reading. "I am now instructing you to take a test to determine the alcohol content of your blood...." At about that point, the man spoke up and said, "Boy, I was blowing these things up before you was born." And with that, he grabbed the mouthpiece and started blowing. Soon the machine began printing out the results, which showed he was well over the legal limit. With the test out of the way, the man asked for his phone call, which he knew he was entitled to. It is interesting how your frequent-flyer offenders know all their rights. If I had a dollar for every time someone told me they knew their rights, I would have several dollars. Not only do they know their rights, they know what my authority is. If there is one thing an officer doesn't appreciate, it's a violator telling you what you can and can't do. That is even more true when that violator is intoxicated to the point they can barely walk.

I escorted the man to the phone. He placed the call and soon received an answer. Although I could only hear his end of the conversation, it was all I could do to keep from rolling on the floor. When the phone was answered, he said, "Martha, well, I'm in jail in Rockford." He paused and then with a startled look on his face and a whining tremble of disbelief in his voice he said, "What? Send you a postcard! Well, if that's all twenty years means to you, then...." I really couldn't concentrate on what else was being said since I was trying so hard to keep from busting out laughing. I didn't think it was the first time Martha had received that phone call. We left the man pleading on the phone with Martha and went about our business.

The next month in district court, the defendant was present; however, his name was not on the docket. I pointed this out to the game warden, and he took the matter up with the clerk. He came back to me and asked what I had done with the tickets. I told him I hadn't done anything with the tickets. I reminded him I had escorted the man to the Intoxilyzer while he was supposed to be handling the paperwork. The blank expression on his face told me he had not written anything. I told him to ask the clerk to hold the cases until the end of court, and we would have the tickets. Somehow the tickets appeared when the case was called. The man pled guilty, and the matter was disposed of.

"Boy, I was blowing these things up before you was born." That is a funny statement but a terribly sad testimony. What about you? How is your testimony? If it's not what it should be, this is your postcard reminding you that only what you do for the Lord will last. Think about it!

It's Not What It Looks Like

IT'S NOT WHAT IT LOOKS LIKE! Have you ever heard anyone say that? In my experience as a law enforcement officer, things are most often pretty close to what they look like.

While working night hunting, my partner, CEO Shannon Calfee, and I were sitting beside a landowners' home watching his pond dam, where some night hunting had recently taken place. One thing I have learned during my thirty-one years as a conservation officer is people trying to illegally kill a deer at night go to where the deer are. If that happens to be in someone's front yard, so be it. I've seen numerous houses shot into by some idiot unleashing a shot in the dark.

At approximately 11:30 p.m., we observed an extended-cab pickup as it moved slowly down the county road. The vehicle eased to a stop, and the beam of a spotlight came out of the passenger's window, illuminating the field across the road from our vantage point. I pulled out into the road behind the vehicle and activated my blue lights. The truck stopped, and the driver immediately jumped out and headed back toward me.

Although the latest trend seems to be to reduce the amount of training needed for someone to obtain a driver's license, I would be a strong advocate for a law enforcement encounter class for drivers. It has been my pleasure to speak at Mississippi State

University each year since 1992. My dear friends Dr. Jeanne Jones and her brother, Dr. Daryl Jones, have allowed me to address their wildlife and law enforcement classes. I have endeavored to provide a comprehensive talk, and one of the items covered is how to respond when stopped by a law enforcement officer. I have pointed out that a good attitude often goes a long way with an officer. However, what I emphasized most was do *not* get out of your vehicle unless and until the officer tells you to. Evidently, folks do not realize an officer is on high alert when approaching a vehicle. This is truer today than ever before. In most of our cases, there is a high probability the folks will be armed. Therefore, someone quickly exiting a vehicle may very well find themselves up close and personal with the business end of a Glock!

Obviously, the fellow I had just stopped gave no thought to what I might be thinking. It's nearly midnight, I've just watched him commit a violation, I'm sitting behind him with my blue lights on, and I suspect he is armed. However, here he comes right at me. With my hand on my pistol, I had no problem giving a very loud verbal command for him to *stop*, and thankfully he had no trouble understanding. I instructed him to put his hands on the tailgate of the truck, and he complied. I quickly patted him down while observing movement in the truck. I told Shannon to watch the driver, and I cautiously approached the cab of the truck.

This was Shannon's first deer season as a CEO. Since our department didn't have an actual field training officer program at the time, and I was the only other "officer" in the county, I was therefore handling his on-the-job training and trying to keep him out of harm's way as much as possible. Approaching on the driver's side of the extended-cab pickup, I observed a woman in the rear seat of the truck trying desperately to stuff a rifle under the seat. While keeping my eye on the man in the front passenger seat, I opened the door and took the rifle from the woman. I told my partner to come up and remove the male front-seat passenger. We found the loaded magazine for the rifle and the Q-Beam spotlight in the front floorboard. After making everything safe, I advised the subjects they were under arrest for hunting at night, hunting from a public road and hunting by aid of a vehicle. The driver immediately told me this wasn't what it looked like. I replied that shining a spotlight from a vehicle sitting in a public road while in possession of a rifle looked like night hunting to me. He replied, "Well that's how you look at it." Nine thousand dollars later, I think they began to look at it the same way!

A question I have posed to many hunter education classes is whether or not the students have ever been in the woods and convinced themselves they were seeing a deer when in fact it was just a bush or a limb. After receiving a show of hands of those who admit having had that occur, I tell the others they either haven't hunted much or they didn't want to tell the truth!

Have you ever said to God, "This is not what it looks like"? We are amazingly good at justifying our actions. We can say, "I know what the Bible says, but..." There should not be a but in that sentence. You may be thinking you haven't done that. You haven't gone against what God said. Be not deceived. We have all failed in many areas. First John 1:8 states if we say we are without sin, we are a liar. We must understand God doesn't play Let's Make a Deal; he says, "Here's the deal." Proverbs says there is a way that seems right unto man, but the end thereof is death. How would we respond if we said, "God, it's not what it looks like," and God said, "Then what is it?"

God is not mocked; He knows our thoughts and observes all our actions. What about your life? Is it what it looks like? Do you know Jesus, or do you know *about* Jesus? God knows which one is true, and we had better know which one is true.

When Jesus said, "Depart from me, for I never knew you," he wasn't talking to someone who just came in off the street. He was speaking to people who considered themselves Christians. We need to take a real look at our lives and then answer the question "Is it what it looks like?" We may not say to God that it's not what it looks like; however, the question is are we saying that to ourselves?

Be Not Deceived

ONE OF THE MOST DIFFICULT ADJUSTMENTS I had to make after going to work as a wildlife law enforcement officer was getting used to being lied to. I was fortunate to grow up in a Christian home and a wholesome atmosphere. It was understood from an early age that lying was wrong and would not be tolerated. I grew up doing my best to tell the truth and expecting others would do the same. I still believe most people are truthful in most situations. However, that statement is not at all true when it comes to conversations between suspects and law enforcement officers.

One of the most blatant examples of bald-faced lying occurred when using one of my favorite game warden tools, the wildlife decoy. It was my good fortune to begin my career when the deer decoy was still relatively new. This meant the fields were ready for harvest, and harvest them we did. I was six days into my career when I first observed the decoy in action. Actually, our first decoy didn't move at all. It just stood there, and people blasted away at it. On my first outing, we garnered four new holes in the small buck. In fact, we got a lot more holes than that. Our first customers pulled up and shot the deer with a sixteen-gauge shotgun loaded with number-six shot. We pulled out behind the vehicle and activated our blue lights, which resulted in a short chase.

Shortly thereafter, another individual eased to a stop and shot three times with a 30-30 rifle. He would have shot it four times, but I reached and took his gun as he aimed at the lifeless statue. Of course, when I turned around and looked at the two seasoned conservation officers standing behind me with unapproving looks on their faces, I realized I might not have learned all I needed to know on our first stop! After they wrote the subject several citations and sent him on his way, we hid back in our hole and waited on the next taker. The officers took that opportunity to tell me I probably needed more than one night of work before I took the lead on approaching armed suspects. Their wise counsel provided me with the skills to safely get through my thirty-one-year career.

The decoy generated many lies since the violators did not know we were present at the time of the violation. More times than I can remember, I have watched as a subject blasted away at the deer and quickly took off down the road. We would run the individual down, only to have them vehemently claim they hadn't shot at anything.

The decoy also generated a lot of lies in another way. People lied about seeing it, about what it did, and about what they did to it. Every season, I would receive many reports concerning a spotting of our decoy. Hunters delighted in telling me they had spied the decoy, and it didn't look real at all. I would ask where they had seen the deer, and inevitably it would be somewhere we had never used it. This mistaken identity no doubt saved the lives of countless animals!

Many hunters delighted in describing how the deer had either stomped its foot or jumped up and down or run in and out of the woods. Most of the stories occurred before we had a decoy that would move at all. (We did eventually get robotic decoys that would put on a pretty good show.)

Some of the biggest yarns were spun concerning what happened when the decoy was shot. I have had many violators tell me "someone they knew" shot the decoy, and the sparks flew off of it. Or they blew the head off of it or the Styrofoam flew everywhere. The truth of the matter was many of the shots directed at the decoy never even came close to it. I guess saying "I missed the game warden's decoy" really wasn't a cool story.

The decoy, of course, wasn't the only source of lies for the game warden. Simply asking someone if they had a firearm in their vehicle would generate multiple lies. Any law enforcement officer who has worked any amount of time knows when you ask an individual if they have a firearm in their vehicle and they reply, "I don't think so," they very likely have a firearm in their vehicle! I had that scenario play out a hundred times during my career.

Approaching armed suspects, some of whom have just violated the law, creates one of the most dangerous law enforcement situations in the country. Those who regularly engage in this type of pursuit are commonly called game wardens. As one might imagine, getting control of a suspect's weapon is a high priority. One of the first questions on many of our stops was "Do you have any weapons in the vehicle?" Of course, there were many times we didn't have to ask due to there being a weapon in plain sight, or we may have just observed the vehicle's occupant using the firearm. However, you would be surprised how well folks can hide firearms, even long guns, in a vehicle. I quickly learned night hunters often would carry their gun between them and the door. A long gun against the passenger door is almost impossible to spot from outside the vehicle. Road hunters often will carry their gun between the seat and the center console. This is easier to spot; however, if the firearm does not have a scope, it can be hidden effectively. Although these were likely places, you might find a weapon anywhere; therefore, you always had to be on guard. I once caught a night hunter whose gun was in the very back of his Jeep Cherokee. It was loaded and ready, but he basically would have to exit the vehicle to retrieve it. However, questioning revealed he had brought the gun in order to shoot a deer if he saw one!

One night—actually it was 3:30 a.m.—county forester Blake Kelley and I had been working night hunting and were headed home. As we eased down County Road 29, we observed a Jeep Cherokee facing us in the ditch on the left side of the road. The headlights were on, and it appeared to be occupied by only the driver. As we neared the vehicle, it bounded up out of the ditch and into the roadway. Anybody out at 3:30 a.m. was a likely suspect, and this driving behavior only added to my curiosity. I told Blake we needed to check this guy out. I didn't know whether he was night hunting, drunk, or—as was often the case—both, but we were going to try and find out.

I pulled in behind the truck and activated my blue lights. The driver immediately pulled the Jeep to the side of the road. I cautiously approached the driver and ordered him to raise his hands where I could see them. Although you are trying to watch everything as you approach, you definitely want to watch the hands. If they are going to kill you, it will be with something in their hands. The driver's hands were empty, and I quickly scanned the front seat for a weapon. I asked the driver, "Do you have any weapons in your vehicle?"

He replied, "No." About the time the word came out of his mouth, I spotted the front sight of a rifle protruding from under a jacket in the rear seat. Without calling attention to the gun, I opened the driver's door and told him to get out. Once he was out, I grabbed him and put him on the hood of the vehicle. I know that may sound abrupt; however, you must realize he had just lied to me about having any weapons, and I wasn't going to take the chance he had another gun up his sleeve. With him secured, I asked Blake to remove the rifle from the back seat. I said to the driver, "I thought you didn't have any weapons," and he replied, "I thought you meant like a baseball bat or something!" I explained to the young man I wasn't really worried about somebody sitting in the driver's seat hitting me with a baseball bat. He stated he had hunted with the weapon earlier in the day and had forgotten it was in the vehicle. The young man was sober, and although I felt certain he was night hunting, I had no real evidence of him doing anything wrong except for giving a stupid answer to a question. And if I locked up everyone who had ever done that, we would be building jails nonstop!

Believe me when I tell you truth was a scarce commodity in the middle of nowhere at 3:30 a.m. and, unfortunately, most of the time. I've been lied to a lot, but I have come to understand some of the worst lies are the ones we tell ourselves. Be not deceived; your sin will find you out.

Fatal Variance
(Now It Has Your Name)

HAVE YOU EVER WANTED TO MELT? Have you wished you could just disappear instead of having to face what was happening? That is the feeling experienced when one stands before the judge in a crowded courtroom and it is pointed out your error has made the difference between a conviction and a dismissal.

During my career, I made a strong effort to work with other law enforcement agencies, including Alabama state troopers, the Coosa County Sheriff's Office, and the Rockford Police Department. Working with officers from these departments no doubt enhanced my law enforcement performance. Although it was no secret our game and fish administration frowned on the practice, I did write several traffic tickets, and working with these officers definitely helped me in that regard.

While accompanying a Rockford police officer, I learned a lesson about accurately writing a ticket that stayed with me. Rockford, the county seat of Coosa County, has a population of about four hundred folks. During most of my career, the police department had only one officer but occasionally two. The jurisdiction is small but does have one state highway and one federal highway running through. Fortunately, the citizens have long enjoyed a low crime rate. You've heard of towns where they roll the sidewalks up at midnight; in Rockford, that takes place at about four in the afternoon. However, we do have one convenience store that stays open until 10:00 p.m.!

While on patrol on US Highway 231, we were traveling north when we met a van with a nonworking headlight. It would be interesting to know how many times an improper headlight has been the probable cause for a traffic stop. My guess would be millions of times, and it often translated into the discovery of multiple violations. We initiated a traffic stop on the van with the intention of issuing a warning for the light. However, arriving at the driver's window, the officer smelled the unmistakable odor of alcoholic beverage emanating from the driver. A couple of quick sobriety tests later, we had the driver cuffed and in the back seat en route to the Rockford Ramada (my pet name for the Coosa County jail).

The officer administered the Intoxilyzer test, and it revealed the driver exceeded the legal limit, which at the time was 0.10 percent. He was placed in jail charged with DUI and improper lights. The case was set for the district court for the next month.

The defendant had hired a local attorney to represent him. When the case was called, the defendant, his attorney, the Rockford officer, and I all approached the judge's bench. The judge advised the man he was charged with DUI and asked how he pled. The attorney advised the judge his client was also charged with another violation and stated he would like to plead not guilty to that charge, the improper light, first.

The judge told the officer to raise his hand and be sworn and then asked him to tell the court what had occurred. The testimony very much resembled the stop and arrest, as it was short and to the point. He explained we had stopped the vehicle for a nonworking headlight and had discovered the driver was intoxicated, and he was arrested. The attorney went to work. Showing the ticket to the officer, he asked if it was the ticket he had written for no headlight. He said it was. The attorney asked him to read the code from the ticket. I knew at this point something was up. The officer read the code, and the attorney again asked if this was the ticket he had written. The officer again affirmed it was. The attorney turned his attention to the judge and explained the code on the ticket was the Alabama traffic law that said it was unlawful to ride a motorcycle without wearing shoes. As it turned out, there was a one-digit difference between the two codes. However, it proved to be enough. The attorney asked if the van driver had in fact been riding a motorcycle, and the officer hesitantly replied, "No." The lawyer turned to the judge and stated his contention that this error represented a fatal variance in the ticket and asked that it be dismissed. The judge promptly dismissed the case.

At this point I was thinking that although we had lost the minor equipment violation citation, we still had the DUI, which was obviously much more significant. This was when I learned a valuable lesson. The attorney again addressed the court and articulated that seeing how our probable cause for stopping the vehicle was no longer valid, he moved that any charge stemming from that stop should be negated. I thought that was a good ploy, but I knew the judge would not fall for it. There was no way he would dismiss something as significant as a DUI just because a simple mistake had been made on a companion ticket. As I said, I learned a good lesson when the judge announced, "Case dismissed." I'm sure a photo of me taken at that moment would have been a great addition to any disbelief definition. I was left standing there with my mouth hanging open. Needless to say, I stored that information away in my file on what not to do.

Anyone who has ever watched an episode of *Law and Order*, *Cops*, or the local news or has read a newspaper has heard of someone who got out of a criminal offense on a technicality.

Unfortunately, it is fairly common. Law enforcement officers are in a difficult profession. Not only because of the danger, long hours, and working in all climatic conditions but also due to the heavy load of stress that accompanies the job. Contributing largely to the stress is the fact people expect the police officer to be perfect. That is a tall order when you are dealing with dynamic situations that demand split-second, sometimes life-and-death, decisions. It's a heavy load. On balance, most officers do a tremendous job. However, everybody makes mistakes, and sometimes they will cost you the case. Sometimes much more.

Like with everything in life, there is normally an exception to every rule, and such was the case with the fatal variance on a ticket. The normal practice of our district judge was to hear all of the criminal cases on the court docket and then have everyone who had received traffic tickets line up and come before the bench. This often meant the traffic ticket folks were about to confront a judge who was testy at best and sometimes totally ticked.

More often than not, the people were their own worst enemies. I can't tell you how many times I have heard a defendant approach the bench and plead not guilty to a speeding ticket. The judge would ask why they pled not guilty, and they would reply they weren't going as fast as was indicated on the ticket. Then he would ask how fast they were going, and they would give him a number only ten miles per hour over the limit. He would then tell them the court found them guilty on their admission of speeding. It happened over and over.

One afternoon I listened as a man approached the bench with his ticket in hand. The judge took the ticket and told the man he had been charged with speeding and asked how he pled. "Not guilty" was the reply. The judge asked on what basis he pled not guilty, and the man stated the name on the ticket was not his. This was when we filled out the tickets by hand, unlike today when our onboard printer spits them out. He continued stating the name on the ticket was Robert T. Jones and he was Robert I. Jones. While examining the ticket, the judge asked the man if he had been driving a blue Chevrolet Impala, and he said he had. He asked if he was the one who had received the ticket, and he replied, "Yes." The judge took his pen and wrote on the ticket and announced, "It now says 'Robert I. Jones.' Now how do you plead?" After a moment, the dejected driver mumbled, "Guilty." The judge didn't miss a beat when he instructed the man to go and pay the clerk. This driver had in all likelihood heard or had been told that if the ticket had an error on it, it would be dismissed. He found out that wasn't necessarily the case.

What about you? Are you thinking you will get off on a technicality? I fear there are many working their way through life thinking on the Day of Judgment they will find a loophole and stroll into heaven. That isn't going to happen. Wouldn't it be awful if you were to stand before the throne of God and He looks at the Lamb's Book of Life and says, "Wait, that's not your name." Galatians speaks very clearly when it says, "Be not deceived; God is not mocked. You will reap what you sow." If your name isn't currently written in the Lamb's Book of Life, you need to change that today. The Lord is willing to write your name there. Think about it.

Decoy Christians
(I Knowed It Wuttn't Real)

"Is it live, or is it Memorex" was a popular slogan back in the day. The gist was something recorded on Memorex tape was so good you could not tell if it was the real thing or a copy. Often it is difficult to know whether something is real or not. Sometimes it doesn't make any difference, and sometimes it makes all the difference.

The deer decoy has been a great tool for wildlife law enforcement. It allows the hunter, the hunted, and the hunter of the hunter to all be in the same place at the same time. My career began in the heyday of the deer decoy, and we made many arrests using it.

Decoys look real and act real but are, of course, fake. Decoys are best when used in a setting where real deer would normally be seen doing what deer do. There is no doubt an art to making an effective setup with a decoy. Although the original decoys were stationary, the deer have really progressed over the years. One of the early versions was set up on a knockdown mechanism that allowed us to drop the deer once it was shot. In response to the deer falling, the violator would often stop, making the apprehension easier for us. The evolution of deer progressed at a quick pace. Soon our deer had tails that would wag and heads that would turn from side to side. Today decoys can appear to stomp their feet and walk. We would often set the deer up and place a live branch in its mouth so that when it turned its head, it would appear it had been browsing on the branch. This proved to be successful more than once.

I was more fortunate than most officers since I lived near the fellow, a retired game warden, who made decoys for all over the country. I got to be in on some of the research and development and was given a couple of prototypes to try. The decoy looked real because it was made from a real deer.

As real as it appeared, the decoy was still fake. Many people (defendants) referred to it as the dummy or the mechanical deer or the robot deer. One of my all-time favorite comments in court was when a decoy shooter stepped up and stated, "Judge, I'm the dummy that shot the dummy!"

It looked like a deer, acted like a deer, and went through the motions of a deer, but it wasn't a deer. For this reason, we had to be specific when charging violators who shot the decoy at night. One charge in Alabama law is "taking deer at night." This charge could not be used when someone shot the decoy since they really weren't taking a deer. They thought they were taking a deer, they were attempting to take a deer, and their intent was to take a deer, but they really weren't taking a deer. Therefore, they would normally be charged with hunting at night.

Many people are surprised to learn the deer decoy was very often used in the daytime. Many "hunters" were what we normally referred to as "window shoppers" or "road warriors" who did their "hunting" from the comfort of their vehicle. During the day, a realistic setup was that much more important.

We once caught a couple of guys we knew had several road-shot deer to their credit. After making two passes, the passenger shot at the deer three times at a distance of sixty yards. The young man's father later told me his son had come home and exclaimed, "It looked good, Daddy! Even you would have shot it!"

To which his dad had replied, "A deer on the side of the road can't look good enough for me to shoot it."

Many times, I have been asked why using the deer decoy isn't considered to be entrapment. The answer to that question is a deer standing in its native habitat doing what it innately would do is a natural occurrence, and no one is being coerced into shooting it. The difference would be if I were to have the decoy set up and then I were to go down the road and tell someone I had just seen a good buck back up the road. In that case, I lured the shooter to a trap.

The decoy looks real, acts real, is where a real deer should be at the time it should be, and makes people think it is real, but it still isn't real.

Unfortunately, I fear the decoy is a lot like many people in the church today. They appear to be Christians, act like Christians, are where Christians are, and make people think they are Christians, but they are only decoys.

While working a decoy detail in Clay County, we had a vehicle slowly approach our setup and roll to a stop. Within seconds a shot split the night. We hastily approached the vehicle and removed the two occupants. As I placed the passenger face down on the hood of the car and began handcuffing him, he stated, "I knowed it wuttn't real."

To this spontaneous exclamation I responded, "Why did you shoot it?"

"I didn't!" was his reply.

"Oh yes you did," I said.

He explained how he had only been looking at the deer, but his gun was messed up, and when you took the safety off it would fire! Later examination of the decoy proved he had been holding a good bead when he took the safety off, seeing how he had hit the deer in the center of the chest!

How do you tell if someone is a real Christian or just a decoy? Just like with a deer decoy, it can be difficult. A decoy Christian may look like a Christian. Well, what does that look like? I think everyone would be hard pressed to nail that down. How do Christians act? They are in church on Sunday and maybe even on Wednesday. They know the routine—when to stand, sit, sing, and pray. They go to the altar and may have been baptized. Since many folks know all that, it can be really hard to tell.

One reason the deer decoy looks so real is because at one time it was a real deer. Folks may look like real Christians, but are they? Could it be this is also the case with the decoy Christian? In Matthew 7, the people who claimed to have done many wonderful works in Jesus's name were the ones he told, "Depart from me, for I never knew you."

In all honesty, it is difficult for us to tell whether a Christian is a decoy or not. But the bottom line is it isn't our job to tell whether or not someone else is a true Christian or a decoy. But it is our job to know what *we* are!

Decoy is defined as a thing or person used to lure or tempt into danger. If we profess to be Christians, yet we are in fact decoys, then woe be unto us. First John 1:6 says, "If we say we have fellowship with him, and walk in darkness, we lie, and do not the truth."

Today we have many "Christians" who, like the fellow in my earlier story, are just taking the safety off. They have no intention of straying from the Lord but are just looking. I can tell you I have dealt with many people who were just looking, and many of them have ended up with their name on a piece of paper that ends up in front of a judge! Christians cannot dabble with sin and still claim to love and have reverence for God.

One day, our names are going to appear before the ultimate judge, whose decision will be just and final.

Romans 14:11 says, "As I live, saith the Lord, every knee shall bow to me, and every tongue shall confess to God. So then every one of us shall give account of himself to God. Let us not, therefore, judge one another anymore; but judge this rather, that no man put a stumbling block or an occasion to fall in his brother's way."

I cannot tell you how many times I have had someone come up to me and tell me they recently saw my decoy. They tell me it really didn't look that real, and they are surprised people are fooled by it. I usually say something like, "Well, it's worked several times," and they eventually go on their way. The interesting part of the story is that we did not have a decoy set up where they said they had seen it!

Has someone seen you and said, "There's a Christian," when in fact they had been fooled? Worse yet, have they viewed our actions and the word *Christian* hasn't crossed their mind? Have we thrown a stumbling block in their path? While it may be difficult for us to tell a fake from the real thing, it isn't difficult for Jesus. We must remember one day we will all stand before God. On that day, the names of the ones He knows will be read. They will not be read from the church roll; they will be read from the Lamb's Book of Life.

Today we need to examine ourselves and ask the question "Am I a Christian, or am I just a decoy?"

Get Him Out of My Sight

YOU MIGHT CONSIDER THE TESTIMONY of someone who was not present when a crime took place to be what would commonly be referred to as hearsay. You would be correct; however, when the judge tells you to share what you know about the situation, the answer is "Yes, your honor."

The Coosa County courthouse towers over the county seat of Rockford as the largest two-story building in town. Originally built in 1858, the structure had to be rebuilt in 1926 following a fire. It was renovated in 1970. During my thirty-one years of law enforcement, I spent a considerable amount of time on the second floor, which houses the offices of the circuit clerk, district judge, and juvenile officer. In the clerk's office, the clerk has an individual office, and the three assistants have desks behind the counter that spans almost the entire length of the room. Between the counter and the wall is a walkway approximately six feet wide. On days when the district court is in session, the line of folks attempting to handle their cases often extends into the main hallway.

As you can imagine, court days were not a good time to try and check on cases or turn in tickets. I usually tried to handle those duties on noncourt days. It was on one of those days I had an interesting encounter with the district judge. As I stood at the counter filling out a warrant, the judge came in with a forlorn-looking young fellow in tow. Handing me a ticket, the judge said the fellow was charged with a management area violation. I looked at the ticket and ascertained he had been charged with operating a vehicle in an area not open to traffic on the wildlife management area. The judge asked me to tell him what had happened. I informed him I was not the arresting officer. The judge looked at me and huffed, "Well, you know what happened don't you?" to which I responded, "Yes, sir."

"Tell me," he said. Although I felt my comments would be hearsay, I knew the judge well enough to know he wasn't interested in my opinion on the law; he wanted to know what had occurred. Therefore, I told him it was my understanding the individual had driven his jeep over some riprap (large rocks) that had been placed along the side of the road to prohibit vehicle traffic and he was sitting in the middle of the rocks when the game warden saw him. The judge promptly found the man guilty and sentenced him to thirty days in jail that would be suspended on the payment of a $250 fine and court costs. The judge told the man to pay the clerk and turned and walked out.

The fellow asked the clerk how much it would be, and the clerk informed him the total would be $449. The fellow pulled out his checkbook only to be informed the court did not accept personal checks. He said he did not have that much cash, and I informed him he would have to go jail. He quickly replied he couldn't go to jail. I told him if he couldn't pay the fine he would have to go to jail.

About this time, the judge walked back into the office and shot me a look that said, "Why is he still here?"

I said, "Your honor, he doesn't have the money."

The judge responded, "Take him to jail." The fellow immediately began to plead with the judge, saying he didn't know it was against the law to drive off the road. At this, the judge exploded (as he was prone to do) and said, "There's thirty thousand laws! Am I supposed to let you break all of them once because you didn't know?" Needless to say, this was a rhetorical question! The judge turned to me and yelled, "Get him out of my sight!" I grabbed the man by the arm and took him directly to jail.

How often does God want to ask us if He is supposed to let us commit every sin before we atone for our transgressions? How often does God feel like saying, "Get them out of my sight?" The Bible says God's spirit will not always strive with man.

While I escorted the man to the jail, he was beside himself with the prospect of losing his job. I attempted to calm him down by explaining his options. I let him know if he could have someone bring the money to the clerk's office before 4:00 p.m., he would be released today. If he couldn't do that, he could request an appeal bond. He immediately wanted to know how to file the appeal. I explained he simply needed to request an appeal bond, and the judge would set one. "The same judge?" he asked in a panic. I told him yes but assured him the judge would set a bond for him. This eased his mind somewhat.

Just like this man, we are guilty, and there will be consequences. While we cannot escape the consequences of our sin, we can in effect be bailed out. Although our sin is a debt we can never pay, Jesus has already made an appeal on our behalf. Our bond has been posted. God sent his only Son so that whoever believed in Him should not perish but can have eternal life. We must decide whether or not to accept this gracious offer of salvation. The choice is yours.

The fellow in this story claimed he was not aware of the law he had violated. I have heard that defense numerous times in my career. While it may have been true a few times, many times it was not. In Proverbs, the claim was made "we did not know this."

The reply was, "Does not He who weighs the heart consider this? Does He who keeps your soul not know it?" The Lord knows the truth, and you know the truth. You now know the choice is yours. We will all live eternally; the question is where. The answer to the question is within your power.

While I am sure the Lord has looked at all of us at one time or another and wanted to yell, "Get him out of my sight," thankfully, He loves us despite our failures. We will never be perfect, but we can be saved. Choose wisely.

Sunday Come-to-Jesus Meeting

IT'S A SMALL WORLD. For many years I served on the National 4-H Wildlife Committee, traveling around the country helping conduct the National 4-H Wildlife Habitat Evaluation Program contest. I served with many folks, with the majority being extension wildlife specialists from land-grant universities. When I first got on the committee the chairman, Dr. Ron Masters, was a professor at Oklahoma State University. While getting to know each other I learned that in an earlier life he had worked as a game warden in Tennessee and was stationed in Chester County, the home of my wife's grandparents. Seeing how I was currently working as a wildlife biologist and CEO, we had a lot to talk about. I also learned he was a Christian, and he spoke of how he did his best to attend church on Sunday, even on days he was working. He said he would often wear his uniform to church and leave from there to go on patrol.

I was fortunate in that working in the wildlife section of our department allowed me to set my schedule for the most part, which allowed me to be off on most Sundays. Although I had to work several Sunday nights, I was normally able to attend church on Sunday.

SUNDAY COME-TO-JESUS MEETING

Ron shared an interesting story about a fellow who he attended church with. As fate would have it, the warden had located some untagged traps on the man's property. I can tell you from experience that isn't a good situation. Ron stated on repeated trips to the area he had failed to find anyone tending the traps. This is not at all unusual. Although traps set on land are required to be checked every twenty-four hours, CEOs can't spend all day monitoring a trap. Therefore, you check the area at the most likely time for someone to check the traps, which is normally early in the morning. Checking at these times had failed to produce any results. When that happens, you change tactics. Ron had checked at all times of the day and had yet to find anyone there.

Checking the area several times, the officer had found evidence someone was checking the trap; the question was when? Eventually, Ron began to notice something interesting. While he would see the landowner at Sunday school, he did not see him at the worship service. Thinking this was unusual, the officer decided he would leave church after Sunday school as well. Lo and behold the two men came face to face at the trap. Ron said it was a very uncomfortable moment as they stood in silence looking at each other. I was surprised when he told me he simply turned around and walked away, leaving the man standing over the trap—alone with his God.

Hunting and trapping are excellent ways to reveal one's ethical behavior. Ethical behavior is not mandated by laws or regulations but by an individual's own sense of what is right. The legendary coach John Wooden is credited with the following quote: "Be more concerned with your character than your reputation, because your character is what you really are, while your reputation is merely what others think you are. The true test of a man's character is what he does when no one is watching."

I'm not going to guess about what you've done or where you have fallen short in your walk with the Lord. I don't need to tell you; you are seeing it in your mind right now. I don't have to speculate; the Bible says all have sinned and come short of the glory of God. It also says forgiveness and eternal life are available.

Embarrassed, the violator in this story quit going to church after this incident. That is understandable. Many of us have difficulty admitting we were wrong. There is a huge misconception that is rampant today. Many folks erroneously believe the church is a place for those who live at the foot of the cross and never sin. The Bible says all have sinned and come short of the glory of God. The remainder of that verse says, *but* the gift of God is eternal life through Jesus Christ our Lord. We don't deserve it, we cannot merit it, but we can accept it. Glory be to God.

Officer Masters went to this man and explained he could give up on God due to his failure in this incident or he could ask God to forgive him and set an example for his son to follow. The man returned to church. The altar can be a place for many things, including redemption, reflection, salvation, and intercession. Whatever you need it for—it's open. The Savior is waiting.

Second Chances

A MULTITUDE OF ARRESTS MADE by Conservation Enforcement Officers (CEO) are the direct result of following up on a "tip" provided by the public. These bits of information range from specific directions to a baited site to a simple observation of a vehicle in an out of the way location. The officer who responds to this information will often be rewarded by making an arrest and will normally continue to receive information from the same source. I've known several good sources of information during my career and one of the best came through again.

During the 2007 spring wild turkey season, my longtime friend and confidential informant alerted me to the presence of a blind built overlooking an area where cracked corn had been placed to attract turkeys. Attempting to attract wild turkeys by putting out bait was unfortunately a fairly common practice. As an avid turkey hunter, the practice is repulsive to me. I cannot understand how anyone who has ever called in and taken a wild turkey can get any enjoyment out of taking one that has been lured in with bait. Just talking about it now I'm getting aggravated!

I contacted my county CEO, who we will call Bud, and told him we needed to go and locate the blind. We met at my home at about 1:45 in the afternoon and headed to the suspect location.

The directions I had were good ones and I did not anticipate any problems finding the blind. We arrived and hid our vehicle up a side road and began walking onto the property. We had gone about two hundred yards when I caught a glimpse, through the woods, of a vehicle parked ahead of us. Taking a few more cautious steps, I observed a camo clad hunter standing beside the truck. I immediately ducked down and motioned for Bud to do the same. I wasn't sure whether or not we had been spotted. I was wearing a mesh camo jacket and hoped it had concealed me. As we stood in the road contemplating our next move, the fellow entered his truck and headed right at us. Run! I said to Bud and we both headed down into the woods alongside the road. We had covered about twenty yards when Bud tripped on a vine and went flying head over heels through the leaves. He bounced off of a small tree and landed in a heap. I dove to the ground and spun around facing the road.

The truck eased along the road and came to a stop right where we had been standing. My heart sank as the truck sat motionless for probably two to three minutes. Believe me when I say it's hard to hide my rather large frame in about four inches of dry leaves. Although I was facing the truck, I could not see the driver and hoped that meant he couldn't see me.

The truck finally pulled away. I sat up and asked Bud if he was okay. He was sporting a pretty good whelp and a cut on his forearm but said he would survive. He dejectedly said, "You know he saw us." I replied I was afraid he had but since I couldn't see him maybe he didn't see us. I told him we needed to assume we had not been seen and hope for the best.

We got up and brushed off the leaves and walked toward the baited area. The blind had been built near the road and wasn't difficult to find. Seeing the configuration of the blind and the type and placement of the bait, I immediately suspected this was an older guy. Experience had taught me the old timers would build their blind behind and beside where they would sit and would have little or no blind material in front of them. In addition, older hunters would often use cracked corn or wheat and would scatter it in the leaves in a semi circle in front of the blind. In contrast, younger violators normally built a fort-like blind in front of them and usually placed a pile of whole kernel corn in front of their location. Based on my observations and many years of experience, I told Bud I thought we were dealing with an older guy, it wasn't his first time doing this and he was probably hunting somewhere else at daylight and coming and sitting on this during the middle of the day. We took a few photos and left the area.

On the way out, I told Bud that although we may have messed things up, we should come back and check it the next day. Before we left, I marked the road so we could tell if anyone had been in the area when we arrived the next day.

The next morning, we were in Coosa County district court for a case where we had charged a man with hunting deer at night and by the aid of bait during the past deer season. Although most cases came to court the month after they were made, the defendant in this case had requested a continuance which had landed the proceedings in the middle of the turkey season. Unlike our turkey case which was based on a specific tip, we had actually sort of stumbled into this case.

After receiving some complaints of people hearing shooting after dark, we were looking for a place to set up our deer decoy. As always, finding a place for the decoy was relatively easy but finding a place where we could sit and work the decoy was proving difficult. We finally located a good decoy site and I eventually spotted a dim woods road we thought might work as a surveillance location. I asked Bud to drive out the road and he stated he knew there was a food plot in the area he had wanted to check out. As fate would have it the dim road led directly to a food plot with a tripod corn feeder standing in the middle of it. We exited the truck and Bud went to check the feeder while I checked around a ladder stand at the end of the field. As I headed back toward the truck, I met Bud at the edge of the field and he said, "this is it." As I was trying to decide what exactly that meant, he added, "This is where they are night hunting, there's corn in the feeder and a rechargeable spotlight in the shooting house." I agreed that sounded like a recipe for night hunting and he said, "Let's get outta here!"

The next day we worked a complaint of someone hunting deer from the county road. The complainant had claimed it was happening every afternoon. The gravel road in the middle of nowhere was a prime spot for some illegal road hunting. However, like many of the "sure thing" complaints we received, the detail did not pan out. Wouldn't you know this would be the day they decided to try their luck somewhere else! If I had a dollar for every sure thing that did not work out I would have several dollars!

Bud was the only CEO in the county at the time and I was by default his "partner." This meant I was back to working 40 hours a week as the private lands wildlife biologist for central Alabama and another 20 or 30 hours assisting him. I enjoyed it, but I admit I didn't have any trouble going to sleep at night. Of course, several of those nights were interrupted by night hunting complaints. Since I had been in the county for twenty years, I received the lion's share of complaints from the public. That was fine with me but it took its toll.

At dark, we ended our road hunting detail. I headed for home and Bud told me he was going to swing by and check the baited stand containing the spotlight. I told him to call me if he found anything. I arrived home and was unloading equipment from my truck when I received a radio call from Bud. He simply stated, "He's in there." I noted the time was 6:04 p.m. Seeing how it was "good dark" around 5:15, I knew the fellow should have already been out. I advised Bud I was on my way and encouraged him to be patient and careful.

As I hurried toward his location I received a radio call but the language was unintelligible. Unfortunately, this wasn't uncommon with our radio system; nonetheless I put the accelerator to the floor and arrived at his location at 6:14 p.m. Seeing how the area was approximately fourteen miles from my house, that was a pretty quick trip.

I found Bud's truck parked alongside the road and I started toward the field. After going a short distance, I passed the truck I assumed belonged to the violator. Looking toward the field I observed the beam of a flashlight in the road ahead. I stepped to the side of the road and waited for Bud and the violator to reach my location. I allowed them to pass by and I followed them out. At the truck, we secured the violator's firearm and I pulled Bud to the side and asked him what had occurred. He said when he was approximately forty yards behind the shooting house, he had observed the trees around the field in front of the shooting house were "lit up" for a few seconds and then everything was dark again. He said he had approached the shooting house and observed the violator sitting in a chair with his loaded rifle resting in a sandbag and his rechargeable spotlight by his side. He identified himself and told the man to exit the shooting house. He escorted the guy out into the field and showed him the corn on the ground under the feeder. The man objected and said he had removed the battery from the feeder two months earlier and he no longer considered the field to be baited. When asked about the light shining on the trees, the suspect denied shining the light and suggested it was probably headlights from a vehicle on the county road that the officer had observed.

After receiving Bud's report, I read the man the Miranda warning and questioned him regarding the corn and the spotlight. The fellow repeated the same arguments Bud had heard earlier. Asked why he was still in the stand almost an hour after dark, he replied he was waiting on the deer to leave the field. The fact the fellow had an unopened lunch and drink in the shooting house gave us the impression he had planned to stay for a while. After a brief discussion, he was placed under arrest for hunting at night and by the aid of bait. He was allowed to sign his own bond and go on his way but not before we took photographs of the bag of deer corn in the bed of his pickup. It was always a good idea to check in the vehicle when you made a baiting case. On several occasions, I found bait inside the vehicle. Although circumstantial evidence, it always seemed to strengthen a case when you were able to tell the judge the bait you found in their vehicle closely resembled that which you found them hunting over. Yep, that always helped.

After the defendant had left, I advised Bud to return to where he had been when he saw the light in the field. I returned to my truck and drove up and down the road with my high beams on to see if he could see any light from the road as the defendant had stated. He could not. We went to the field and took photographs of the area under the feeder that was void of grass. This was in contrast to the remainder of the field, which was covered with forage six to eight inches high. These photos provided a graphic rebuttal to the violator's argument there had not been corn on the ground for two months and would figure prominently in court.

Court was scheduled for 9:00 a.m. with the Honorable Carlton Teel presiding. Prior to court, the clerk had received a call stating our defendant had car trouble and would be late. Court began and when we reached the defendant's name on the docket he still had not arrived. Therefore, he was passed over to be called later. This disappointed us in that we were anxious to check our turkey bait.

The defendant finally arrived and eventually his case was called. The defendant approached the bench and pled not guilty. Bud testified to what had occurred and when he finished the judge asked the defendant if he had any questions. The man stated he did not agree there was any corn on the ground prior to Bud shaking the feeder and making it fall out. I provided the photos of the bare dirt under the feeder and the lush vegetation in the remainder of the field and the judge found the defendant guilty on both counts. We hurriedly left the courtroom and headed toward the baited area.

We soon arrived and once again hid our truck. A check of the road revealed a vehicle had been in the road since the day before. I was cautiously optimistic as I followed Bud easing up the road. However, the optimism quickly diminished when just as we neared the point in the road where we had run from the day before, Bud gasped, "Oh no!" and fell to the ground. What? I asked and he said, "The guy is standing beside his truck and he looked straight at me." My heart sank. It was bad enough to think we had messed things up the first time, but to have received a reprieve and now messed it up on our second chance was sickening. Getting two chances at someone on bait was a luxury that didn't occur very often.

"Are you sure he saw you?"

"I think so."

Frustrated, Bud said let's go and check him. I countered that the only thing we would be able to do was to tell him the area was baited and he could not hunt here again until the bait was gone for ten days. As we contemplated what to do I stepped up and looked toward the truck and could not believe my eyes. The camo clad man was walking away from us; gun in hand, toward the bait. It was hard to believe but it appeared we had once again dodged a bullet.

We waited for ten minutes and followed the man up the road. I had gone maybe a hundred yards when I spotted the fellow who had stopped at the top of the hill. Bud and I ducked down and watched as the man stood motionless for at least two minutes. He again started walking toward the bait. We waited five minutes and again took up the pursuit. We were now walking along a new white gravel road. We had to move slowly to keep the noise to a minimum. It is amazing how loud something moving across gravel is. I have heard vehicles easing along a gravel road from long distances on a quiet night and even footsteps on gravel are loud. We did our best to stay on the edge of the road as we slowly pursued our violator. Soon we were within about fifty yards of the blind. A turkey load from a shotgun can do tremendous damage at fifty yards. Things were getting serious.

Walking up on someone in a turkey blind is probably one of the most dangerous things a conservation officer does. Although you always try to approach from a safe direction, you never know for sure which way the person may be facing. You don't know whether or not they are watching you approach and you don't know what they may be capable of. By the grace of God, I've approached a lot of blinds and shooting houses and have lived to tell about it.

Fortunately, the gravel played out before we reached the blind allowing for quieter travel. Unfortunately, this blind was situated so we had to initially approach from the side and the violator could likely see us before we could see him. I didn't like this set up. I decided a diversion would be helpful and might provide us a bit more safety. I picked up a rock and threw it so it would fall out in front of the blind. I hoped this would attract the violator's attention. As soon as I threw the rock, I ran down the road, which placed me directly behind the blind. I knew due to the construction of the blind; the man would be facing away from me. However, that was only true if he was in fact sitting in the blind and there was no guarantee on that. I inched toward the blind and when I was twenty yards directly behind it I announced "state game warden." This received no response. I waited on the violator to either stand up or in some way acknowledge my presence but nothing happened. I continued to close in on the makeshift hideout. My heart was once again sinking when I was within ten feet of the blind and still did not see anyone in it. "How many times are we going to mess this up?" I asked myself.

When I was five feet from the blind, I finally saw what I realized was two camo covered knees. "Put your hands up" I snapped and the hands immediately came up. I moved closer and told the man to hand me his gun. I took the twelve-gauge shotgun, unloaded it and handed it to Bud. I ordered the man to stand up and let me see his license and permit. He found his license and told me the landowner's name that had given him permission. I asked if he knew why we were there. He hesitated and said, "Because I'm hunting over a baited field." I told him to gather his stuff and we escorted him to his truck.

At the truck, Bud began writing a citation while I questioned the man and searched his vest and truck. I must admit I was somewhat pumped up not only that we had caught the guy after so many near misses, but also by the fact I had been dead on about the guy. The man was 63 years old. I asked if he had ever been arrested before and he replied he had not. However, I detected his "No" answer wasn't heartfelt. I gave him a really good "it's time to tell the truth stare" and again asked if he had ever been arrested. This time he shook his head yes. For what? I asked "the same thing" was his beleaguered reply. The man was placed under arrest and allowed to sign his bond and go on his way. I normally don't adhere to the saying that it's better to be lucky than good, but in this case, we most definitely had the luck with us!

While this was a great catch, it unfortunately proved to have a major detrimental impact to my law enforcement career. After learning this guy was a repeat violator I told Bud I felt in addition to charging him with hunting by the aid of bait we should also charge him with 9-11-236 the state law prohibiting hunting in closed season. Seeing how we were in the middle of the turkey season, Bud responded with a befuddled look. I explained that years earlier, at the urging of the National Wild Turkey Federation, the state legislature had amended our hunting in closed season law to read:

> Any person who hunts, takes, catches, captures, kills, or has in his or her possession or who attempts to hunt, take, catch, capture, or kill, any bird or animal protected by law or regulation of this state except during the open season when same may be hunted, taken, caught, captured, or killed shall be guilty of a misdemeanor and, upon conviction, shall be punished by a fine of not less than two hundred fifty dollars ($250) nor more than one thousand dollars ($1,000) and, at the discretion of the court, may also be imprisoned in the county jail for not longer than six months.
>
> *It is provided further that any person who hunts, takes, catches, captures, or kills, or attempts to hunt, take, catch, capture, or kill, <u>a wild turkey in an illegal manner</u> or during the closed hunting season, or has in his or her possession a wild turkey killed during the closed hunting season or taken in an illegal manner,*

shall be guilty of a misdemeanor and upon conviction shall be punished by a fine of not less than two hundred fifty dollars ($250) nor more than one thousand dollars ($1,000) and, at the discretion of the court, may also be imprisoned in the county jail for not longer than six months.

Like many officers, Bud had never heard of this part of the law but agreed we should charge the man.

At the next district meeting, in front of the entire district, the captain asked Bud how he charged a hunter with hunting in closed season when the season had been open for two weeks. Bud took the opportunity to reveal to everyone present the portion of the law I had revealed to him. This was not a problem until he also revealed that I "the biologist" had told him about the law. He told me the captain immediately blew a gasket and said he would not have a "biologist" telling an officer what to do. Bud said he tried to explain I had not told him what to do but had made him aware of what the law said. However, the captain was incensed. I ended up taking a lot of flak and basically being ostracized by many of the game wardens at the request of the captain. Although I continued to work enforcement and was able to maintain a relationship with several of the guys who I had worked with for years, my relationship with the enforcement section took quite a blow. This was difficult to accept. I had worked extremely hard to cultivate a good working relationship only to see it torn to shreds by an insecure captain. It was this "us versus them" attitude that hindered the effectiveness of our department evidently from day one until today in some districts. I would survive it, but it wasn't as fun as it could have been.

Fast forward ten years. In my position as the central Alabama private lands wildlife biologist I was trying to cover thirty plus counties. While I enjoyed working closely with landowners wanting to manage the wildlife on their properties, it deeply cut into the time I had to work enforcement. Since the case outlined earlier had occurred, Coosa County had undergone quite a turnover in the area of conservation enforcement officers. We now had a wildlife biologist who had transferred into the enforcement section and another young officer who had transferred into the county one year earlier. The officers were young and eager to locate violators which is what a county with a lot of hunting needs. The old captain was long gone and we were once again working together when we could and sharing information. The 2016 turkey season found both of the CEOs really getting after it.

Early in my tutelage I learned a lesson about persistence. My mentors, game wardens Earl Brown and Hershel Patterson were as different as daylight and dark in the techniques they employed. However, one thing they agreed on was if you wanted to be successful when working bait, you needed to be persistent and patient.

At the beginning of the last week of the spring turkey season I received a call from CEO Stewart Abrams seeking some information. He explained he had located a lot of turkey bait on a property and was needing to figure out how to access the property without being seen. Stewart knew I enjoyed assisting whenever possible and since I was coming up on thirty years in the county I was often familiar with problem properties. As fate would have it the property he was trying to access was adjacent to a property I had hunted regularly several years earlier. I told the officer which key would open the lock on the gate and gave him instructions on which road would carry him directly to the baited property. He assured me he would be waiting on the culprit the next morning. I wished him luck.

The next morning found me standing on a ridge at daylight waiting on a turkey to gobble. Fortunately, the bird did gobble and soon thereafter got to go for a ride in my truck. Although I was overjoyed with taking my first bird of the season (with only a week left) I was definitely hoping Stewart had been successful as well.

I sent Stewart a text (Oh how things had changed) telling him I had killed a bird and asking if he had been successful. He replied, "Not yet." I had explained to him earlier a favorite technique of turkey baiters was to hunt somewhere else at daylight and move to their baited area for the middle of the day. I kept in touch with him through the day, however at the end of the day no one had shown up. I praised the officer for his perseverance and encouraged him to stay with it. He told me it appeared the area had been freshened up with cracked corn. I took the opportunity to tell Stewart that in my experience cracked corn was used by older guys and assured him the violator had not freshened the bait without the intent to hunt it again. I shared with him the story about how Bud and I had caught an older guy using cracked corn and how we were lucky enough to get a second chance at the guy. I again encouraged him to stay with it.

The young officer worked the bait for five days with no luck. On the sixth day, I received a call from Stewart. He asked if I had had any luck turkey hunting. As I began to respond he blurted out, "I caught two on the bait, a husband and wife." There was no disguising his excitement. I told him that was great and said let's hear the story. He explained how he was about to give up hope after he had watched the road since before daylight and had failed to see anyone entering the property. Before he left the area, he decided to check the entry road one more time and lo and behold someone had driven in the road. He quickly hid his vehicle and hurried toward the first baited spot.

As he eased up to the blind he was a little surprised to see not one but two people sitting inside. He identified himself and took their guns and unloaded them. He told me the couple was very cordial and admitted to having put the bait out. After writing both of them for hunting by the aid of bait and failure to possess a turkey harvest record they signed their bonds and told him they knew he was just doing his job.

One of the things I always wanted to know was the names of the violators and I asked Stewart for that information. He stated it was a seventy-three-year-old guy and his wife and the man's name was Luther something. This time I cut him off before he could say the last name by blurting out, "Johnson!" I told him that was the same guy Bud and I had caught! Stewart said the man had admitted he had been charged with the same thing in the past. Yeah twice, I added. The pair appeared in court and pled guilty to each charge and paid fines and court costs totaling $1,000.00

I hope you were able to stay with me through all of these interrelated stories. It actually covered a decade although it seems as though it happened last week. Life flies by and we will definitely make mistakes. I'm thankful we get second and third chances. However, one day will prove to be our last and there will be no more chances. Are you ready for that day? On that day, every knee will bow and every tongue will confess Jesus is Lord. If you need another chance to get things right, Jesus offers that to you today. Make the most of it. Choose wisely. Choose Jesus.

Bubba Plans to Kill 'Em

IT WASN'T TOTALLY UNUSUAL for a landowner to want to take matters into their own hands when it came to dealing with wildlife law violators. I could easily understand the emotion; however, it really wasn't worth killing the folks.

During the mid-1990s, it seemed like every time my phone rang during the deer season it was either a landowner with a complaint or one of the county game wardens telling me of a complaint they had received. With a lot going on, we tried to share information so whoever might be working would be able to better respond when called. I answered the phone, and Game Warden Hershel Patterson said, "I'm on the way to get you."

I said, "Okay," and hung up the phone. Knowing it would take Hershel at least twenty minutes to get to my house, I began getting my uniform on. I met Hershel in the driveway, and we were on our way to what proved to be a very interesting call.

As we pulled out of the drive Hershel asked me if I had ever heard of Bubba Bluff. I was not sure whether that was someone or some place. Either way, I was not familiar. He explained Bubba was one of a rough bunch of brothers, most of whom were either dead or in prison. Bubba had called to report some shooting after dark near his house.

It took us about fifteen minutes to reach the Bluff residence. Therefore, this complaint was now nearly an hour old. Judging by past experience, I had serious doubts we would find anyone still in the area, but I had been wrong before. We pulled up to the house, and a man came out and met us on the porch. Hershel introduced me to Bubba, or Mr. Bluff, as I would refer to him. Mr. Bluff was a big man, over six feet tall and stocky. He appeared a lot less sinister than what I had conjured up from Hershel's description; however, I had been fooled before. He shook my hand and started on a diatribe I could hardly believe. He said, "Well Hershel, I hated to call y'all. I was just going to kill 'em, but my wife kept on at me saying, 'Don't kill 'em Bubba, don't kill 'em,' so I called you." I must admit I was taken aback not only by what was said but also by the matter-of-fact way it was stated.

He continued, saying he had a ten-gauge shotgun loaded with buckshot, and he planned to kill them when they came back by his house. He said the road that passed in front of his house was not passable, and they were likely stuck in the muddy road, seeing how they had yet to come back by. I was thinking they better hope they stay stuck if they don't want this guy to blow them away!

"What exactly did they do?" Hershel asked.

"They went right down the road there and shot!" Mr. Bluff exclaimed. He added, "They ain't got no business shooting around my house." Hershel told him it was our job to handle it, and he did the right thing calling us.

We returned to Hershel's Crown Victoria and started down the road. I had a couple of burning questions for Hershel. The first one was, "Was that guy serious?"

Hershel looked at me and said, "Yeah, he was dead serious."

I wasn't sure whether or not the pun was intended. This shook me up a little bit. I knew he had sure sounded serious, but that was pretty extreme. I asked Hershel, "How far do you think we will make it down this muddy road in this car."

"As far as we can," was his dry reply. At this time, some officers had four-wheel-drive trucks, and some had cars. Hershel had driven the Crown Vic for years and knew what the car could and couldn't do.

We had not gone very far when we spotted a vehicle sitting at an awkward angle on the edge of the road. We eased up to the vehicle and got out. The road was indeed very muddy, and we were doing our best not to slip while keeping an eye on the two men and two women in the vehicle. The driver exited the car and said he was glad to see us. The guy struck me as a used car salesman from the 1970s, complete with the slicked-back hair and sleazy smile. We asked what had happened, and he said they had just been out riding around and had gotten stuck. I looked at Hershel, and he nodded his head. That signal meant for me to take the lead in talking with the subjects. He was an excellent training officer. He would let me take the lead and let me run with it without interfering. If I got in over my head, he was there to bail me out. I learned a lot working with him.

I asked the driver if he had any weapons in his vehicle, and he assured me he did not. I told him we weren't just out riding around; we were responding to a night hunting complaint, and seeing how his was the only vehicle on the road, it led us to believe he was the culprit. He denied any knowledge of any wrongdoing and said a pickup had pulled up behind them earlier. I shined my light down the road and told him I would have thought a truck would have left some tracks in the mud. He did not respond. I told him I had something else I needed to tell him. Seeing I had the attention of all involved, I informed them the man who lived at the end of the road where they had shot earlier had debated about whether or not he should call us when he heard the shot. I said, "Luckily for you, he decided he would because his first idea was to wait and kill you when you came back out." This left the people with an astonished look on their faces. Before they could think too much about it, I added, "I'm not kidding." I let that sink in for a minute. I could tell the wheels were turning in the driver's head as he contemplated their situation.

There is an art to questioning people, and it has a lot to do with timing. Sometimes rapid-fire questions are called for, while at other times you need to let things hang in the air for a bit. Thinking he had had enough time to consider his situation, I looked at the driver and asked, "Where's the gun?"

He did not hesitate as he replied, "It's in the trunk."

I said, "Let's get it."

He opened the trunk and I retrieved the lever-action 30-30 rifle. I put it in our car, and Hershel and I began writing tickets for hunting at night.

After we had explained the bonds and allowed the defendants to sign them, we began trying to get their car out of the mud. Using a combination of Hershel pulling and me and the male passenger pushing, we were able to get them back in the roadway. The fact that I, the apprentice, was given the opportunity to push—which, of course, left me covered in mud—was not lost on me. Hershel told them to follow us out and not to stop when we passed by the house at the end of the road.

As we neared the Bluff residence, I told Hershel to turn on our blue lights since I sure didn't want Bubba mistaking us for the night hunters. The car stayed glued to our bumper until we hit the paved road and they took off. The quartet came to court the next month, pled guilty, and paid their fine and court costs. I will never know if they ever understood how close they came to paying the ultimate price that night. It was truly a close call.

Can you see yourself in this story? Bubba's first thought was to take matters into his own hands. How often do we do that? While that may be fine for many day-to-day situations, what about life-and-death decisions? This was well on its way to being a life-and-death situation. Fortunately, Bubba's wife convinced him to go to the authorities for assistance. That decision may have saved the outlaws' lives, in addition to keeping Bubba out of prison. What about you? Do we venture into life-and-death decisions without consulting the ultimate authority?

I have attended church literally my whole life. One of the saddest things I have routinely observed is women having to assume the role of the head of the household when it came to spirituality. I admire these women. The statistics and the consequences concerning fathers not attending church are horrific. Are you like the man in this story? Is your wife advising you to consult the ultimate authority to make a decision that has eternal consequences?

We will answer for all we've done or failed to do. It will happen, and when it does, it will be everlasting—too late to make a change. The folks in this story were one trigger pull away from eternity. None of us know which day will be our last. The choice is ours. Choose wisely. Do it today.

Will I Get My Gun Back?

"I THINK THEY JUST SHOT MY HORSE!" Those were the frantic words I heard when I answered the phone at 10:30 p.m. on Saturday night. I did not need any further explanation. I knew who "they" were: night hunters. I had been spending a lot of time chasing "them" lately. I told my friend I was on the way, and I began pulling my uniform on.

It was highly unusual for me to be at home on a Saturday night during deer season. For the first seventeen years of my career, I basically worked every weekend from November through January and sometimes February. As an area biologist with law enforcement responsibilities, I worked management area hunts every Friday and Saturday of the deer season. More often than not, we would work the hunt during the day, followed by working night hunting for most of the night. It wasn't at all unusual to work twenty-eight hours or more in two days.

Within minutes I was in my truck and speeding toward the area of the complaint. I was very familiar with the remote area where the caller had heard the shot. Although only a couple of miles from my house as the crow flies, the area was approximately five miles by road. As I neared the field, I slowed my speed and went into observation mode. I observed a small pickup pulled off to the left side of the county road. I cautiously eased up behind the vehicle and, noticing it was unoccupied, began looking for the occupants. I noticed the vehicle's tag. In Alabama, before the onslaught of vanity license plates, the first number of a license plate indicated what county the vehicle was registered in. This truck carried a thirty-one county tag, which meant I would probably soon be writing a ticket.

For many years, people from this county seemed to be the majority of the hunters all across the state. Unfortunately, many of these folks had a propensity to violate the game laws. As a matter of fact, when I first arrived in Coosa County, my two game warden mentors both told me if I spotted a vehicle with a thirty-one or a fifty county tag, I would probably need to write a ticket. I was sort of taken aback by this blatant stereotyping. However, it wasn't long until I found what they said to be the truth! Call it profiling if you must, but I was sitting behind a vehicle with a thirty-one county tag at 10:40 p.m. with the information that someone had just shot three times.

Not seeing anyone, I exited my truck and cautiously approached the vehicle. Like most aspects of conservation law enforcement, this was a dangerous activity. You knew someone was here somewhere; someone had just shot, yet you couldn't see anyone. I eased up to the passenger side of the small pickup and shined my light into the front seat. There I observed two high-powered rifles. While standing by the truck, I began to hear voices and quickly realized they were coming from the adjacent pasture. Looking into the field, I soon observed three individuals walking toward the road. The fact I had seen two rifles in the truck and now saw three people was not lost on me. Keeping the truck between us, I scanned the individuals for a weapon but did not see one. Surprisingly, the trio appeared not to notice my truck sitting behind theirs; however, I knew my arrival surely had not gone unnoticed. I shined my Maglite on the three and told them to stop where they were. I asked if they had any weapons, and they replied they did not. They added the usual comment received from folks found out of the vehicle at night: they had only stopped to use the bathroom.

Although I have dealt with multiple subjects in this type of situation many times, it isn't the safest situation. Therefore, I was glad to see the county game warden, Earl Brown, pulling up on the scene. It turned out the landowner had also called Earl. Together we solicited some identification from the three subjects. We asked what brought them to this pasture in the middle of nowhere a hundred miles from their home at about 11:00 p.m. One of the subjects replied they were on their way to see a friend who lived nearby but had stopped to use the bathroom. I asked if they normally went one hundred yards off the road and across a fence to use the bathroom. Getting no response, I tried another question. I asked the name of the friend they were going to visit. Evidently it wasn't a good friend, seeing how they couldn't come up with his name. I asked if it was their custom to go and visit people whose name they didn't know at eleven at night.

As they were trying to explain the situation, the landowner arrived. Earl and I briefly spoke with him and decided he should take a spotlight and see if he could locate his horse or anything that had been shot in the pasture. He pulled down into the field, and we returned to the suspects. While Earl was explaining to them they were lying and it was obvious to us, I began scanning the area around their vehicle with my flashlight. Soon I spied something shiny, and closer investigation revealed three spent 30-06 hulls. I picked up the hulls and then retrieved the rifles from the truck. As fate would have it, the rifles and the spent cartridges were both 30-06 caliber.

The landowner returned and told us he had located the horse, and it had not been shot. While we were thankful the horse was okay, we had hoped the fellow would locate a freshly killed deer in the pasture. Although the circumstantial evidence was strong, it was still circumstantial. Earl read them the riot act and told them they might as well come clean. They replied they hadn't done anything, and Earl responded by telling them they were under arrest for hunting at night.

This move took me by surprise. Although I shared the thought they were obviously guilty, I knew the law was clear: since the violation did not occur in our presence, we really couldn't arrest them without a warrant. However, seeing how Earl had been doing this for fifteen years before I started, I figured he knew what he was doing. He told them we would be keeping their firearms as evidence. I added we would send the guns and the spent hulls to the forensic lab, and they would be able to tell us with 100-percent accuracy which gun fired the shells. When I finished explaining this, one of the subjects excitedly looked at me and asked, "When you do that, will I be able to get my gun back?" It was all I could do to keep from busting out laughing as he, without realizing it, had just pointed a finger at his companion. We finished the necessary paperwork and allowed them to leave. We took a look around the field with the spotlight, and in the back corner we located a freshly killed doe. After taking a couple of pictures, we gave the deer to the landowner and went on our way.

Firing the "other guy's" gun produced the expected results, and we were well prepared when the case came to court. The case was called, and the three defendants approached the judge's bench. After the judge listed the charges of hunting at night, hunting from a public road, and hunting by the aid of a vehicle, he asked the subjects how they pled. One of the subjects, the gun owner, asked if the judge would appoint him an attorney to represent him. The judge gave him the necessary paperwork, and the cases were set aside. The defendant soon returned the paperwork to the judge. After reviewing it, the judge informed the man he could afford his own attorney. It was obvious the defendant didn't agree with the judge; however, the tone the judge had used let him know he was on his own. The judge called for a short recess.

During the recess, one of the local attorneys approached the defendant and told him he would represent him for $250. The man told him he didn't have $250. The lawyer asked if one of the rifles we had brought into the courtroom belonged to him. He stated the 30-06 rifle with the scope on it was his. The attorney told him if he would sign the gun over to him, he would represent him. Reluctantly, the subject signed the gun over. The attorney briefly conferred with him. This made me a little uneasy in that I was afraid the attorney's first question would be whether or not we observed his client shooting the deer. However, there was nothing that I could do about that now. I just hoped for the best.

When court resumed, the cases were once again called. Although the attorney had only agreed to represent the one defendant, all three subjects approached to have their cases heard. Many times, I have seen this type of "borrowing of legal counsel" when multiple subjects were charged in the same incident. As it turned out it wasn't the best idea in this particular situation.

The attorney approached the bench and stated he represented the subject. Then, in a move that shocked me almost as much as the defendant, he stated, "We plead guilty, your honor." The defendant's jaw went slack as he looked at the attorney in disbelief. The judge stated the court would accept their plea. The judge proceeded to levy fines and court costs in each case. The other two defendants, seeing the writing on the wall, pled guilty. They received the same fine and costs as the first subject; however, unlike him, the second subject *did get his gun back!*

WILL I GET MY GUN BACK?

When the accomplice in this story asked, "When you do that, will I be able to get my gun back?" what he was really asking was, "Where will I stand when the truth comes out?" That is a question each of us needs to consider. There is a day coming when everything will come to light. Where will you be standing then? The answer is you won't be standing; you'll be on your knees. Will you be praising or begging? That decision needs to be made today!

Something I hope you noticed at the start of this story was the caller never identified himself, yet I immediately headed toward the location. Obviously, I recognized the voice on the other end of the line. What about you? Does Jesus recognize your voice? Maybe more importantly, do you recognize His?

Jesus gave His life to serve as your advocate. Who will stand beside you in the court that will seal your eternity? If you haven't accepted His offer of salvation, today is the day!

Get That Light Outta My Face

ALTHOUGH MANY OF THE MORE INTERESTING STORIES during my career came from enforcement encounters, the wildlife management segment also provided some interesting situations. Since we were wildlife biologists and conservation officers, it was often difficult to separate the two. Sometimes they were one and the same.

One of the many wildlife management activities we performed was the collection of deer to determine conception dates. This normally involved several nights riding in the back of a pickup with a rifle and spotlight and trying to shoot adult does. Unfortunately, due to several years of nonharvest of the female segment of the deer herd, our sex ratios were skewed. On some properties, the doe-to-buck ratio was estimated to be twenty to one. This type of situation takes its toll on a deer herd. Since there are too few bucks trying to service the does, many does fail to get bred when they should. Does continue to come into estrus each twenty-eight days and are often bred months later than what is optimum, resulting in late birth dates. These deer often exhibit low body weights and poor antler development. I have aged thousands of jawbones from harvested deer. The late breeding was evident in that many of the deer that should have been eighteen months old were in reality only thirteen or fourteen months old. This diminished the health of the herd and kept them from reaching their potential.

In order for the fawn fetuses to be large enough for us to accurately age and thereby determine the conception dates, we normally had to wait until April to begin the collection. Unfortunately, this meant the springtime vegetation green up had occurred, and visibility was significantly diminished. Ideally, you would have fawns being born in May; however, we were seeing fawns born as late as November! While we would occasionally spot a doe in an open field, they were often in the woods, providing us with a challenging shot.

Late one night, wildlife biologist Gene Carver and biologist aide Dunnie Harrison, from the Hollins WMA, which was located about twenty miles north of my area, were assisting me in central Coosa County on a piece of private property 1,300 acres in size. The property was secured by locked gates at each entrance, and the private wildlife biologist for the property had assured us no one would be allowed on the place during our collection. The property had a lot of steep terrain and was a difficult place to find good shooting opportunities. There was one main road through a large valley, and the rest of the roads were up and down steep hills.

We had made a comprehensive trip around the farm and were coming back through the valley when we spotted a deer high up on a hill bordering the road. Gene and I were in the back of the truck, and Dunnie was driving. We tapped on the roof, our high-tech signal for Dunnie to stop, and I found the deer in the scope and shot. The deer went down but was not dead. I was trying to line up a second shot but the deer was now low in the vegetation and I was having trouble seeing enough to shoot at. We were having Dunnie move the truck up and back while we tried to spot the deer.

While this was going on, I happened to look behind us and spotted a pickup truck coming along the road. The vehicle pulled to within about forty yards of our truck and stopped. I knew there was not supposed to be anyone on the property, but obviously somebody didn't get the memo. I turned my spotlight on and shined the truck and saw there was a female driver and a male in the passenger seat. As I looked at the pair, the woman stuck her head out of the window and yelled "Get that light outta my face!" in a very clear and belligerent tone.

I thought that was a little strange, seeing how she had just driven up on two guys in the back of a pickup, both of them holding spotlights and high-powered rifles and with pistols on their sides. I handed my light to Gene, asking him to keep the light in her face, jumped off the truck, and headed toward her vehicle. As I walked up to her window, it was immediately obvious she had now had the opportunity to better assess the situation. Her first words were, "We won't tell anybody. If you'll let us go, we won't tell anybody."

Although she already wore a worried look, I would pay good money to have had a video of her face when I said, "It's too late for that, sister." Even though it was nighttime, I could plainly see all the color immediately drain from her face, and I thought I might have heard the sound of vinyl puckering!

"What are you doing here?" I asked, and she responded they were just riding around. She again added they would not tell anybody if we would let them go. I asked her who had told her she could ride through the property, and she said no one had said she could, but she worked at the house on the property, and they sometimes rode across the property at night. Although I think it was because he may have been intoxicated, the male passenger had not uttered a word. I shined my light in his face, and his look told me he was a mix of drunk and terrified. I figured I had better let these folks off the hook, and I informed them who we were and what we were doing. Surprisingly, this had little effect, as the woman again told me they wouldn't tell anybody. I told her that would be best, and she needed to turn around and go out the way she came in. She immediately slammed the truck in reverse and got gone. I returned to the truck and shared with Gene and Dunnie what all had transpired. After a good laugh and a lot of "What was she thinking?" we climbed the mountain and found the deer I had shot.

One day we will all face what the woman in this story faced. We will be hit square in the face with the Light of the world. The Light of the world, Jesus, is coming back. One day every knee will bow and every tongue will confess Jesus is Lord. The Light will be brighter than we have ever seen. The judgment will be swift, sure, and accurate. Are you ready for that? If not, today is the day of salvation!

I Don't Want to Go to Prison

ALL WILDLIFE IN ALABAMA is held in a public trust for the use and benefit of the citizens of the state. That is one of the founding principles of our country and is dramatically different than that of most other countries. This is considered a sacred trust. In the early morning hours following Halloween in 2006, this trust was desecrated by the egregious activities of wildlife law violators. Fortunately, a law-abiding citizen learned of these events. Recognizing that these outlaws were stealing from him and every Alabamian, the individual contacted me. That contact and the investigation it prompted resulted in justice being served.

The morning of November 1 found me in my Alexander City office. October was always a busy month for wildlife biologists in Alabama. The month was full of landowner tours, planting wildlife openings, meeting with landowners, and the start of bow season. Therefore, the first of November was a busy day of catching up and submitting the mound of reports and other paperwork that were required to keep things running. I was deep into my monthlies when I received a visit from a young man. I had known the fellow, the oldest son of a coworker in another agency, since he was a boy. He was now out of high school and attending the local junior college. He shared with me that he wasn't sure what he needed to do, but he felt compelled to come and tell me several deer had been killed illegally and were currently in the backyard of a residence in Alexander City. He did not have any details other than he had seen the deer in the back of a truck and knew they were not there the day before. I thanked him for providing the information and assured him we would look into it. I wasn't sure what we might have, but since he reported there were several deer in the truck, I felt certain it would at least be an over-the-limit violation. Realizing that gun deer season was still three weeks away and that few archery hunters killed multiple deer in a day, I felt there were probably other violations involved.

I immediately contacted Tallapoosa County CEO Jeff Brown by radio and learned he and Sgt. Michael East were at a district meeting in Prattville about seventy-five miles from me. I relayed the information I had to Jeff, and he told me he would tell his supervisor and be on the way as soon as possible. I told him I would be glad to assist in any way.

You may wonder why I didn't immediately go to the location I'd been given and start arresting folks. That is a good question with a difficult answer. Evidently, when our department came about in 1907, there was a rule instated that wildlife biologists and conservation officers were never to get along and/or work together. Even after wildlife biologists were given enforcement authority, getting the two groups to work together was difficult. When I was hired, I was told part of my job would be to mend fences with the officers in the county and to work with them. Wanting to do a good job, I went to work trying to pull things together.

Although I achieved a good measure of success, it was at great cost. I would soon learn that neither side really wanted to work together, and that went all the way to the top in Montgomery. Fortunately, the two officers in the county where I was assigned were willing to give me a chance. They taught me a tremendous amount, and I soon was making cases (arrests) on my own. I made more cases in my first year of work than many of our longtime employees had ever made. It wasn't long until my case numbers were rivaling those made by the officers in the district. While some of the officers would work with me, because I was willing to work, others, including the captain, resented my enforcement work. At times, it was almost humorous. At a statewide meeting (something we used to have before the budget couldn't handle it), while talking with officers from another area of the state, I would chime in about some night hunting or baiting case I had made, and they would look at me in disbelief and then ask if the arrest occurred on the management area. I would reply no, it was out in the county. They could not believe it was true.

There was always friction between the wildlife and enforcement sections, and I always hated it. So that is why I called the officers in Tallapoosa County: I did not want them to think I was stepping in front of them. Let me point out I always enjoyed a good relationship with Jeff and Michael, and we never had a problem working together.

In just a minute, my radio beeped, and it was Jeff returning my call. I anticipated him saying he was on the way; however, I could tell by the tone of his voice something was wrong. He stammered around a little as he informed me his supervisor felt it was more important for them to stay at their meeting than to come and answer this call. He was apologizing and telling me if it was up to him, he would have already been on the way. I knew that was true because Jeff was a conscientious officer and always worked hard to do a good job. He told me he would answer the call when they returned that afternoon. I told him I felt certain the evidence would be gone by then, and I would go ahead and check things out.

Although I had been given the address, I was not familiar with that part of town, so I contacted the Alexander City Police Department (ACPD) and requested their assistance. I soon met ACPD Sgt. Easterwood (now the assistant chief), and we proceeded to the location, arriving at 8:30 a.m. We immediately found eight dead deer in plain view. Seven deer were in the beds of three trucks, and one was on the ground. Initial examination revealed that seven of the eight deer had been killed with a rifle within the past few hours. This was of major interest, since it was nearly three weeks until the opening of gun deer season. We repeatedly banged on the front and rear doors of the residence but received no response. With the magnitude of what we had found, I knew I needed some help with the investigation, so I contacted wildlife biologist Gene Carver and requested he come to my location. Gene worked in an adjacent county and said he would be on the way. I began taking photographs and gathering evidence. A check of the vehicle license plates revealed no current owner information on file.

When Gene arrived, we again attempted to get someone to the door. Getting no response, we determined we needed to come up with a name and thought we could likely obtain one from paperwork visible inside the pickup that contained five deer. After a discussion on probable cause and a brief talk with the county district attorney, it was decided that obtaining a search warrant for the truck would be the wisest course of action. Although I had searched a lot of vehicles, I had never before obtained a search warrant to do so. Since most of our arrests were on view, meaning we saw the crime happen, and since we were often removing weapons for our safety, we normally did not need a warrant. However, this day I was not in "my" county, and when the district attorney (DA) said he thought a warrant would be best, I had to take that advice. I went to obtain the warrant, while

Gene remained at the scene preserving the evidence. Sgt. Easterwood had to return to his regular duties, and I thanked him for his assistance.

While I was at the DA's office, a young woman arrived at the house and informed Gene she lived there with her boyfriend. Gene explained he was there in response to the numerous dead deer on the premises. She said she had no knowledge about the deer. She told him she was going into the house, and he accompanied her onto the porch. When she opened the door, he observed two men asleep on couches in the front room.

I arrived a few minutes later. As Gene and I were discussing our next move, a large disheveled guy opened the door and stepped out onto the porch, followed by another guy who obviously had not gotten enough beauty sleep. We would soon learn these were indeed our culprits, whom we will call Elmo and Peewee.

We immediately separated the two and told them we needed to ask them some questions. I took Elmo and read him his rights, while Gene did the same with Peewee. I asked simply what was going on with all the dead deer, and Elmo replied his friend Peewee had killed them and had brought them to him to clean and put in the freezer. I asked when he had killed them, and he said he did not know. I continued the questioning and soon began ramping up the intensity. Elmo continued to attribute everything having to do with the deer to his counterpart, except for the big nine-point buck. He emphatically proclaimed the buck was killed legally with a bow and arrow, and he was going to enter it in the big buck contest at the local archery shop. Having already examined the wounds on the deer, I knew it had been killed with a rifle, but I didn't let on.

For someone with eight dead deer lying in the yard during the closed season, Elmo was pretty talkative. Having conducted numerous investigations, I had learned if a suspect wants to talk, let them talk. After listening closely to his answers, I began to point out several inconsistencies in the story. As often was the case, the suspect became confused concerning his own story. I knew it was time to bring the hammer down. I replaced my inquisitive questioner face with my stern interrogator face and told him I was tired of the lies and was ready to hear the truth. Elmo began to tear up and told me he knew it didn't do any good to lie. I reassured him that was true. He stated he, Peewee, and another friend, whom I will call Clueless (and you will soon understand why), had killed the deer the previous night. He began giving a detailed account of the incident, during which he stated he did not want to go to prison. When I told him these charges were misdemeanors and wouldn't send him to prison, he responded he was on felony probation. He was right in thinking this information might change things. I contacted the Tallapoosa County Sheriff's Office and learned Elmo had outstanding warrants for probation violations, failure to pay, and failure to appear. Before he had completed giving his statement, deputies arrived, and were waiting to take him into custody.

With Elmo on the way to jail, I conferred with Gene concerning Peewee's statement. He stated Peewee was sticking to the story he had killed the deer earlier that morning from the loft of a barn located behind his mother's house, and he had left the gun at home. I told Gene I had received a full confession and written statement from Elmo, and I thought we could get the truth from Peewee.

We brought Peewee around from the other side of the house, where Gene had been questioning him, and stood behind his brand-new pickup that had five deer in the back of it. I asked him where he had killed the deer, and he stated he had killed all of them behind his mother's house early that morning. I asked how he killed them, and he replied he shot them with his .260-caliber rifle. I stood there for a moment as if deep in thought. I told him it seemed odd to me that five deer, a spike and four does, would stand still long enough for him to kill all of them.

I let that hang in the air as I moved over and began examining the wounds on the deer. I turned to him and asked where his gun was. He immediately said he had left it at home. He did not know that while he was asleep earlier, we had done our best to look through the window of his truck, and, although it was covered by a pair of coveralls, we had a sneaking suspicion the rifle was in the back seat of the truck. I asked Peewee if I could look in his truck. He thought for a moment and said he would rather I didn't. With considerable flare, I ripped the search warrant out of my pocket and handed it to him while advising him it was a warrant to search the truck. The young man was noticeably shaken and stood in silence while I opened the rear door, moved the coveralls, and removed a loaded .260-caliber rifle, a spotlight, and three knives. I told Peewee we had just proved he was a liar, but it was now time for him to tell the truth. Ultimately defeated, he gave a detailed statement that mirrored the one received earlier. I should mention here that also found in the truck was the bill of sale showing that the truck had been purchased within the last week for over $43,000. I think I may have mentioned to him that any vehicle used during night hunting was subject to being confiscated and condemned. Statements and other evidence in hand, we left the scene.

A lot had occurred, and the adrenaline rush was tremendous. I contacted Jeff Brown and Sgt. Michael East and brought them up to speed on the results of the investigation. I told them the third suspect, Clueless, needed to be located. Later that day, Michael contacted me and said he had ascertained the location of the Clueless residence. After a short discussion, we decided to try to talk with the subject that night.

I traveled to Newsite in northern Tallapoosa County and met Michael and went to the residence. After introducing ourselves, we advised Clueless we wanted to ask him some questions. He was open and frank in his conversation and told us he went spotlighting and hunting with Elmo and Peewee. When asked if they had any luck, he enthusiastically reported he had killed a doe and Elmo had killed a nice nine-point. He went on to say it was his first deer, and his buddies had rubbed the blood on his face. He was so excited I almost hated to ask him if he knew hunting at night was against the law. When I did ask him, his demeanor didn't change, and he replied, "Yeah, I know." He gave a detailed written statement. Clueless, oh yeah.

Armed with statements and overwhelming evidence, Michael and I obtained arrest warrants for each subject for charges of hunting at night, hunting from a public road, and hunting by aid of a vehicle. Elmo was arrested at the Tallapoosa County jail, and Michael arrested Peewee and Clueless at their residences.

The cases were heard by the district court judge in Dadeville in December. In the face of the evidence, each defendant entered guilty pleas. Citing the severity of the violations, the judge handed down the maximum fine in each case, for a total of $3,000 for each defendant. In addition, he revoked the hunting privileges of each defendant for three years.

While I received substantial assistance from the ACPD, the Tallapoosa County district attorney's office, and wildlife biologist Gene Carver, these cases would never have been made without the contact from a local ethical hunter outraged by this horrific abuse of the resource. This is an excellent example of what can be accomplished when the public works with law enforcement. I later nominated the tipster, and he received a monetary reward through the Alabama Wildlife Federation Operation GameWatch program.

As I mentioned in this story, confronted with the reality of the situation, Elmo began to cry during questioning. Although I had seen it before, it wasn't an everyday occurrence. I thought there might be more going on than merely a game and fish violation (or a handful of them). The fellow made two interesting statements, the first being "I know it doesn't help to lie" and the other being "I don't want to go to prison." I responded I believed honesty was the best policy and that these misdemeanor charges likely would not send him to prison. His response, that he was on felony probation, was no doubt a game changer.

Obviously, my initial assessment of what his punishment would be was wrong, seeing how I didn't have all the facts of the case. I fear many folks in and out of the church are wrong when they consider the consequences of their sin. I fear they underestimate the cost that must be paid. The wages of sin is death, and for those who do not know Jesus as their Savior, an eternity in hell awaits them.

As it turned out, this fellow was sent to prison. That's bad, but it's nothing compared to an eternity spent separated from God. A lot of folks walking around "free" today are actually prisoners of sin. You can change that this day. Today is the day of salvation.

As I write this article, it has been a couple of weeks since I testified before the grand jury concerning a fellow I arrested for multiple hunting violations and felony drug charges. I must admit the situation made me feel a little old, seeing how the assistant district attorney who presided over the cases was the "kid" who had provided the tip that led to the earlier outlined cases many years ago! Oh, how time flies. Don't put off today what needs to be done today. Tomorrow isn't guaranteed.

We're Ready to Go!

As VEHICLE ACCIDENTS GO there wasn't really a lot to it. However, the officer whose head bounced off the back glass didn't see it that way. The way he reacted you would have thought I had done it on purpose. I felt his hollering and rubbing his head was sort of making a mountain out of a mole hill. I was a little groggy but that wasn't from the impact.

I have said many times one of the most dangerous aspects of the job of a conservation enforcement officer (CEO) is something most people probably would never think of. That is the fact you often go from being asleep to driving down the road at eighty mph in a span of less than fifteen seconds. I have had several officers tell me they never go to sleep while working through the night. This is commendable. I doubt it's true, but if it is, it's commendable. I admit, without reservation, I often went to sleep while working night hunting details. That does not mean I wasn't working or I was neglecting my duties. Although many people doubt what I am about to share with you, I promise you, like everything in this book, it is the truth. While working night hunting, I developed a technique, not purposefully mind you, to where I could both sleep and yet be aware of what was going on around me. Even to the point I could answer questions, hear my number called on the radio and pinpoint shots I heard while sleeping. My longtime coworkers, CEO Hershel Patterson and Lt. Jerry Fincher, my wife and several others I have worked with can verify this.

There was often good reason for my need to sleep while working night hunting. When I went to work, our chief told me there had been little to no enforcement done on the wildlife management area (WMA) I was assigned to and it would be my job to turn the situation around. I was instructed to get with the conservation officers in the county and learn the ropes and get to work. I did just that. One thing I did not realize prior to my employment was the statement I signed saying I would not work over forty hours a week was evidently only a formality and wasn't to be taken seriously. At least that was the way it seemed. After getting to know the officers, I begin working with them regularly in addition to performing my duties on the WMA. This meant there were many days I would begin work at 7:00 in the morning and would finish around midnight only to repeat the same scenario the next day. Seventy to eighty-hour workweeks were not uncommon for the first several years of my career. We worked all the time and we caught a lot of people.

During the deer season, I was required to work a management area hunt almost every weekend of the nearly three-month long season. This meant each Friday and Saturday I traveled to the WMA at either 4 or 7 a.m. depending on whether or not I had a helper at the time, and would stay there until at least 6:00 p.m. Since the weekend was also the busiest time for night hunting violations, I would often work until midnight or later each night. This meant in many cases I would accumulate nearly forty hours of work in two days. This type of routine was played out for ten weeks from late November thru the end of January. Therefore, it wasn't difficult to fall asleep while sitting in the dark in the middle of nowhere waiting to hear a shot.

We're Ready to Go!

As I mentioned, many times I had been asleep yet heard and actually pinpointed where a shot had come from. Being able to accurately pinpoint shots was a valuable skill for a conservation officer. It often would allow you to quickly intercept the vehicle from which the shot was fired and sometimes would allow you to pull into the field while the night hunters were retrieving their kill. Being young and gung ho I preferred this method, however I quickly learned there were two schools of thought on how an officer should respond upon hearing a shot in the dark.

My veteran training officers emphasized that only in rare circumstances should you leave your position upon hearing a shot. Their thinking, based on experience, was you were more likely to catch someone if you would sit tight and allow the hunters to pass your location. When they did you could pull out behind them without your lights on and follow them until they committed a violation in front of you. Or if they had shot close by you could pull out behind them and stop them from behind which was much safer than running toward them and making a head on stop. This method had merit and produced a lot of arrests. Depending on the situation we employed both techniques. That is until our department banned us from running without headlights. As it turned out this wasn't a safe technique. Can you believe that? Someone in the Montgomery office decided driving down the road in the pitch dark without our headlights on wasn't safe! They were always coming up with something that made it harder to do the job!

Unfortunately, while working night hunting after two long days on the WMA, my sleep would sometimes be too deep to hear a shot. This was rare but it did happen. My most memorable deep sleep event occurred at the end of a marathon weekend. Wildlife Biologist Gene Carver, my counterpart from nearby Hollins WMA, and I were working night hunting on county road fourteen in Coosa County. We had both worked the last two days and were worn out. However, night hunting was going on and we were out there "working" it. This night we were in the Richville area working with the local CEO. Due to a lack of good hiding spots, we decided to sit in the same dim road. I backed my truck into the hole and the CEO backed in in front of me. The night was uneventful and it didn't take long for us to doze off. Actually, I did more than doze off; I was in a deep sleep.

Awakened by my snoring, Gene roused up and decided we were wasting our time. He shook me awake and said we weren't doing any good and we might as well go home. I agreed. I cranked the truck dropped it in gear and "BLAM!" I rammed the truck which was parked about six feet in front of me. Now I was awake. I put the truck in park and opened door. I saw the officer coming out the door of his truck rubbing the back of his head, which had just bounced off the back glass. He yelled what the "heck" are you doing? To which I replied, "We're ready to go." Come to think of it, he didn't park in front of me anymore!

What about you, are you ready to go? One thing that is obvious is tomorrow isn't guaranteed. During my career I responded to many death scenes. This included car accidents, suicides, murders and accidental deaths. The victims ranged from eight years old to eighty. Unless the Lord returns first, we will all die. Are you ready to go?

Never Give Up

BAITING CASES often took a tremendous amount of shoe leather (legwork). Bait was located in several ways, but no matter how we learned of bait being in an area, it usually took a considerable amount of walking to find it. Midway through my career, a new tool became available that significantly changed how bait was located. Around 2005, the enforcement section issued the game wardens GPS units. The units had many uses; however, my favorite use was for marking bait while flying in the departmental airplane. The bait was often easy to spot from the air; however, it was sometimes difficult to find once back on the ground. The go-to feature on the GPS allowed you to select the waypoint, and the unit would direct you to it. I found using the feature was much akin to going on a treasure hunt.

One day in 2006, our conservation enforcement officer (CEO), whom I'll call Bud, contacted me and said he had marked a baited site, and we needed to try to find it. He was overly excited when he explained to me the area appeared to have a trough feeder with five hundred pounds of corn in it! Now that's a lot of corn.

During this time, we only had one CEO in the county, and although I worked a full week doing my wildlife section duties, I also served as his partner. We got together and began working to locate the baited area. Having made or assisted on over one hundred baiting cases in my career, I thought I had observed people hunting over bait in almost every imaginable configuration. I've seen people watching a bait pile while perched thirty feet high in a tree stand and while lying in a depression in the ground. I've seen people hunt from a shooting house, a hunting cabin, and off the front porch of their home. I apprehended people hunting over bait in the morning, midday, evening, and the dark of night. However, the setup Bud and I found on the property we called the Crawford tract was unlike any I had ever seen. Little did I know it would turn out to be unlike any other case I had ever worked.

Once we figured out where the feeder was, we realized it was much like many other baited areas in that it was fairly easy to locate yet not easy to access without being seen. The property bordered a well-used state highway, which increased our odds of being seen entering the place. Therefore, we needed to come up with an alternative route to reach the site. Going through our collective set of over three hundred keys, we finally located the one that would open a gate that allowed us to drive within a couple of hundred yards of the back side of the property.

The first thing I noticed about the property was there were POSTED signs on almost every tree. Although the property was small in size, it had approximately three hundred yards of road frontage, and there were over thirty POSTED signs along the road. Fresh, multiple NO TRESPASSING signs were usually an indication that we needed to take a look at the area. I remember one of my mentors, Hershel Patterson, telling me several times that new NO TRESPASSING signs and a new lock as big as your head usually indicated something nefarious was taking place. The NO TRESPASSING sign on the post just under the basketball goal in the yard of the house on the property was definitely something we would consider a clue.

We entered the property and soon were standing at the trough full of corn. It didn't have five hundred pounds, but it was full. The feeder was approximately seventy-five yards from a house on the property. The Crawford tract was a seventeen-acre parcel of land, and at various times while working the property, there were four stands located around the bait.

Although the feeders on the property were your run-of-the-mill trough and hanging feeders, there was something very different about this setup. The stands were unlike any I had ever seen. They were wooden ladder-type stands made in an A-frame configuration. They were four feet wide at the base and tapered to approximately one foot wide at the top. While the shape of the stands wasn't that unusual, it was very odd to me that the stands were only six feet off the ground. However, that still wasn't the most unusual aspect of the setup. The thing that really threw me for a loop was the placement of the stands in relation to the feeders. As stated earlier, I had observed my share of stands over bait. I had caught bow hunters sitting within ten yards of a pile of corn and rifle hunters two hundred yards from a feeder. Yet, this was a new one. The six-foot-high stands were six feet from the feeders. I must admit I still have not been able to figure this out.

My first thought was it could be a bow hunting setup; however, having bow hunted for years, I could not see how anyone would think they could draw a bow undetected while only six feet off the ground and six feet away from the animal. I considered that a crossbow would not have to be drawn, yet just having a deer that close didn't make any sense to me. I could not get past the question of why anyone using any hunting method would sit so close to a feeder that they would be hit by the corn when the feeder went off. That was literally the case. A five-gallon-bucket feeder with a slinger on the bottom was hanging from a tree with a short stand propped against the base of the tree. The feeder literally slung corn onto the seat of the stand.

I began to do some investigation and learned the property owner was an elderly man nearly eighty years old. I also gathered he was in very poor health. I wondered whether this could be the reason for the low stands and close feeders. If it was him, it would not be the first time an eighty-plus-year-old man had been arrested for hunting over bait in the county. Further investigation revealed this man was in no condition to leave the house; however, it also revealed the man had two sons. One lived locally and the other in a town approximately fifty miles away.

The surveillance of the property continued throughout the deer season. The property was situated along a major highway I traveled on a very regular basis. I had wrongly assumed I would simply keep an eye on the property, would see a vehicle parked there, go in, and apprehend the subject. That was not to be the case. To say I passed the property a hundred times during the deer season would not be an exaggeration. In addition, Bud and I alternated walking into the property from the back side, yet we never found anyone on the property. There was always evidence someone was actively visiting the area, yet we never saw anyone. This was baffling to say the least. After checking the property at all times of the day, we decided it must be hunted at night. However, checking the area at night failed to turn up anyone. This pattern of checking the property from the road and by walking in went on for nearly four years!

In 2007, Bud would be joined in the county by a partner we will call Tom. Tom was taken to the property and brought up to speed on the situation. Bud then transferred to another county. He was soon replaced by another officer we will call Chuck, who was shown the property and told the story. These two officers continued to check the property regularly, and I continued to drive past the property on a regular basis. But all of this was to no avail.

Finally, with the 2009 bow season only three days old, Chuck decided to check the property once again. He walked in on the property and found the feeders once again full yet with no hunters in place. As he turned to leave, movement toward the house caught his eye. He eased behind a tree and watched as a large man made his way toward the trough feeder. It was thirty minutes before dark and the man carried a green plastic chair and had a rifle slung over his shoulder.

Once he was close enough, Chuck stepped out and identified himself. He took the rifle and asked what the man was doing. The man was hard pressed to explain the rifle in bow season and the corn-covered area. Chuck explained he was under arrest for hunting by the aid of bait and in closed season. The officer asked the man why he wasn't bow hunting, and he replied he loved deer meat and did not want to miss one. The next week the man pled guilty to both charges and paid fines and court costs totaling $938.

What about you, do you have perseverance? This case is all about perseverance. Just like life. God calls on us to persevere. First Corinthians 15:58 reads, "Therefore, my beloved brethren, be ye steadfast, unmovable, always abounding in the work of the Lord, forasmuch as ye know that your labor is not in vain in the Lord."

Some might say this was a lot of work for not a lot of return. I would have to disagree. Having this case come to fruition was very sweet. I did not know all the wildlife officers in the state, but the many I did know and worked with didn't have much give up in them. Jesus requires the same from us who call ourselves Christians. The Bible says, "Let us not be weary in well doing: for in due season we shall reap, if we faint not."

When things get tough, we must remember the words from Philippians, "No, dear brothers, I am still not all I should be, but I am bringing all my energies to bear on this one thing: Forgetting the past and looking forward to what lies ahead, I strain to reach the end of the race and receive the prize for which God is calling us up to heaven because of what Christ Jesus did for us." Never give up!

There Was My Hat

I COULD HEAR THE PANIC in the woman's voice over the phone. I didn't know what the problem was, but I could tell she definitely had one.

Several times in my career I received calls concerning a lost hunter. Most of these were on the wildlife management area, but some were not. For some reason, people only seem to get lost on the coldest, most miserable nights.

As my rear end hit my chair at the table, the phone automatically rang. I answered to find our county juvenile officer on the line. She excitedly explained how a friend had gone hunting on her father's property and had yet to return. She also stated the man had recently had back surgery, and they were quite worried something had happened to him. I told her I would be en route to her dad's house and see what was up. Fortunately, the majority of these types of calls normally ended with the hunter coming out on a road somewhere, cold, hungry, and embarrassed. However, you never knew, so I was soon on the way to the property.

I arrived and spoke with the landowner, who told me where he thought the man had been hunting. While we were talking, another vehicle pulled up, and then another. I asked the landowner who these people were, and he said he wasn't sure, but his daughter had called the sheriff's office (SO), and they had said they would send someone. Obviously, the SO had contacted the local volunteer fire department, and within thirty minutes, the property was crawling with people. Now let me say I very much appreciate people who will volunteer their time and talent to serve others. In a rural county like ours, volunteers provide all of the fire protection and emergency medical services. The people are dedicated and work long and hard to help others. However, in some situations, a large crowd of people isn't really what is needed.

The first problem we encountered was the debate over who was in charge. I had already devised a search plan; however, it did not call for fifty people! Soon the sheriff arrived on the scene and decided he would take over and run things. Realizing nothing was going to happen fast, I decided to take a couple of folks and move around to the other side of the property and see what we could find.

By the time we got started, it was close to midnight. As I had feared, the large number of people had become a stumbling block. This was evident from our vantage point, from which we could hear two different groups yelling, thinking each other was the lost man yelling back. Around 1:00 a.m., I heard a shot, which, unless it came from one of the rescuers, was a good sign. I had an idea where it had come from and began moving in that direction. Unfortunately, the area we were attempting to navigate was extremely thick and filled with briars that had never seen a man. It was slow going trying to find our way. Soon we heard another shot, and we were close. So close we could hear the man respond to our calls when the other rescuers weren't responding to them! We found ourselves fighting our way through the thickest tangle of briars I think I had ever encountered. When we finally broke through, we found the man lying on the ground. Other than being totally exhausted, he was okay.

There Was My Hat

After I had ascertained the hunter wasn't injured, I looked at him and asked if he had a permit for the property he was now on. The astounded look on his face was priceless. I followed up by saying, "You didn't think I came all the way in here for nothing, did you?" That brought a smile to the man's face, after he realized I was only joking with him.

The man had walked until he was totally given out and was now unable to walk. We called for some of the rescuers to bring in a stretcher to carry the fellow out. While waiting, I asked the guy what had happened. He stated he had been hunting and had killed a deer. He had to trail the deer a short way and had not paid attention to where he had gone. He began dragging the deer out and became disoriented. He said he had dragged the deer for what seemed like hours but finally had to leave it and try to find his way out. After walking a long way without recognizing any landmarks, he came to a log and sat down. While there he took off his hat and placed his head in his hands and tried to figure out which way he needed to go. He soon got up and took off walking again. He said he walked for a solid hour when he came to a log and sat down. He said, "I looked around, and there was my hat!" He stated he realized he had walked in a circle for a solid hour.

The stretcher soon arrived, and we began the long, hard task of getting the guy out of the woods. The sun was coming up when we came out on the road. After having to help carry the man on the stretcher, I was once again appreciative of the volunteers who had come to assist.

I told this story many times in hunter education courses. The first rule of being lost is not to panic. The second rule is to admit to yourself you are lost. I was very fortunate in my career that each time I searched for a lost person, they were found unharmed.

This guy had to do exactly what every one of us has to do. He had to admit to himself he was lost. We must admit we are lost without Jesus as our Savior. Many folks today are a lot like this guy: they are wandering in a jungle, and it isn't easy to maneuver through. This fellow tried all he knew. He tried looking for landmarks. He listened for flowing water or for traffic. He walked as far as he could. But in the end, all he attempted failed. It is the same with us. We will never achieve salvation on our own. Jesus said, "I am the way, the truth, and the life: no man comes to the Father, but by me."

You may be lost, but you can be found. Reach out to Jesus. Do it today.

You Can't Straddle the Fence

A GOOD INFORMANT IS LIKE GOLD for a law enforcement officer. Receiving "good" information is often the key to making good arrests. Notice I said "good" information. Unfortunately, a lot of the info we receive is of little or no value. However, over time you learn who can provide good information, and you learn to really appreciate it. One November afternoon, I received a call from my former partner, retired game warden Hershel Patterson, telling me he had heard some shooting up on the mountain in front of his house and didn't think anyone was supposed to be hunting there. The shooting was on his neighbor's property, and I knew there were only a couple of permits out, and I held one of them. I contacted CEO Shannon Calfee, and we responded to the call.

Upon arrival, we located a Chevrolet pickup parked on the property adjacent to the mountain property. While at the truck, we heard a shot southeast of our position. The shot sounded as if it came from the neighboring property. We drove around to the county dirt road that split the posted property. I exited the vehicle and headed toward where we had heard the shot. After traveling an old road north and west for a couple of hundred yards, I crossed a branch and entered an overgrown clear-cut area. I traveled approximately one hundred yards through the clear-cut but could not continue due to the impenetrably thick vegetation. I again heard shots up on the mountain due east of my position and definitely on the posted land. The hunters shot numerous times and were talking loudly. I estimated I was approximately one hundred yards below them; however, I could not continue through the thicket. I exited the property via the route I had entered, and Shannon and I returned to the truck on the adjacent property to wait.

Shortly thereafter, we heard the subjects approaching. In the dim light, we could make out three subjects, each carrying a firearm. We approached the subjects and asked them to raise their hands. We checked each subject for any weapon they might have in addition to their shotguns. I asked to see their licenses and permits. The two adults handed over licenses and permits for the property their vehicle was parked on. The third individual, a juvenile, handed over a hunter education card and a permit. When I asked if they had a permit for the property they had actually been hunting on, the older fellow quickly stated they were hunting on his uncle's land. I informed him I had reason to believe they had been hunting on the adjacent property. The fellow responded they had only crossed the line to retrieve a squirrel. Seeing additional questioning was going to be in order, I decided it was a good time to advise them of their rights. I read them the Miranda warning, and they stated they understood.

We separated the adults, and Shannon and I asked the talkative fellow whose property he was hunting on. He replied his uncle's land. I asked how much hardwood was on his uncle's property, and he admitted there wasn't much. I explained I realized the adjacent property was much better squirrel habitat, and I could see why he would have been there hunting. I asked if he had killed the squirrels in his bag in his uncle's pasture. He hung his head as he said no. I asked if he was actually hunting on the adjacent property, and he admitted he was. I asked did he have a permit for that property, and he again gave a dejected no. He asked if the landowner's son-in-law had been hunting over there and called us. This type of question was very common. People always wanted to know who they might be able to blame for their misfortune. It rarely crossed their mind they might be solely at fault. I told him the son-in-law had not contacted us, and he stated he knew they didn't want anybody hunting over there. I made a note of that comment, seeing how it would work well in court. I have often encouraged young officers to develop their listening skills. Violators often inadvertently offer incriminating statements that make the difference in court.

I spoke with the other adult hunter and asked if he had been hunting on the adjacent property, and he replied he had crossed the line to retrieve a squirrel. I asked did he have a permit for the property, and he replied he did not. He then utilized an excuse I had heard several times. He said he thought you were supposed to retrieve game you shot. I told him that was true, and, as a matter of fact, we had a regulation that said you are required to make every effort to retrieve game you had shot. I waited for him to nod his head in agreement, and I said, "I take it you are familiar with that regulation?" He replied he was familiar, and I followed up, saying, "The last line of the regulation reads, 'Nothing in this regulation permits or requires a person to enter upon the land of another for the purpose of retrieving game without the permission of the landowner.'" With that, the look on his face went from one of hope to sheer defeat. I prepared a written statement and asked them if it was correct. They stated it was and signed it.

As we were completing our contact with the hunters, the owner of the pasture property, the uncle of one of the hunters, arrived on the scene. As he sat in his truck, I identified myself to him. I found his first question to me appropriate when he asked if the boys had got across the line. I replied they had. The man began to attempt to explain the line wasn't necessarily straight. I was preparing to inform the fellow that it wasn't very hard to tell the difference between pasture and mature hardwoods when the nephew spoke up and said, "It's okay Uncle Fred, we did it." The landowner again started pleading the case, and his nephew again stated, "It's okay Uncle Fred, we did it, we were over there." We told the subjects we would be in touch with them in the near future and left the scene.

On the way home, I explained to Shannon why we did not go ahead and arrest the violators. I told him if I didn't miss my guess, Uncle Fred and others would probably show up for court, and we had better have all our ducks in a row. Although we had technically observed them on the property by our sense of hearing, since we had not actually seen the guys on the property, it would be best not to make an on-view arrest but to obtain warrants for the two adults for hunting without a permit. This would be based on our observations and their signed statement, which placed them on the property without a permit. I asked Shannon to obtain the warrants and contact the men and tell them we would meet them at the forestry office in Hanover Saturday morning at 11:00 a.m. to handle the paperwork.

Saturday morning, as we neared the forestry office, I told Shannon if he didn't slow down we would run past the office. He replied the defendants had told him they did not know where the forestry office was and would meet us at the local convenience store. I told him that was a bad idea. He asked why, and I told him if I didn't miss my guess, he would soon find out.

We arrived at the store and the two men and one man's father were waiting for us. We exited our truck and greeted the men. I showed the men the warrants and told them we needed to have them sign a bond, and they could be on their way. As I began to explain the bail bond, the father of one of the defendants interrupted and said, "I've talked with an attorney, and he says you can't do this." If there is one thing a law enforcement officer doesn't appreciate, it's someone telling you what you can and can't do. I assured the man what we were doing was legal and proper and told him he should bring his attorney with him to court if he wanted to contest the charges. As I once again began to explain the bond, the man stated he had talked with the probate judge, and he had also said I couldn't do this.

I hoped Shannon was now beginning to understand why you don't try to serve a warrant in a convenience store parking lot. If it wasn't bad enough that this twenty-six-year-old man had brought his daddy to speak for him, now we had ten people surrounding us and supporting the man's contention that we couldn't do what we were doing. Although I did not fear any reprisal from the crowd, it did not help matters that we were surrounded by folks sympathetic to these poor boys that we were doing wrong. I knew this had gone far enough, and it was time to get a couple of things straight. I told the elder man we had a warrant in hand and there were two options at this point. His son could either sign the bond or we could take him to jail. The man again stated the probate judge had said we couldn't do this.

As he was still pleading his case, I grabbed the son, a fairly large fellow, and spun him around and put his chest down on the hood of the vehicle. Simultaneously, I pulled my handcuffs from my belt and began placing them on the man. Almost in unison the father and son both yelled, "We'll sign it, we'll sign it." I looked the man right in the eye and told him I wanted him to understand the probate judge didn't tell me what I could or couldn't do. I asked if he understood, and he replied he did. I asked the son if he wanted to sign the bond, and he enthusiastically indicated he did.

I let the man up, and he signed the bonds. I advised him of the court date and told him to bring his dad, his attorney, and the probate judge with him. Shannon and I completed the other fellow's paperwork and left the parking lot. I asked if he now understood why you didn't serve warrants at the convenience store, and he said it would never happen again.

The court date came around, and I was ready for a trial. However, when the judge skipped over the defendant's names and moved on down the court docket, I knew that wasn't a good sign. At the next recess, I approached the judge and asked if the cases had been settled. He replied they had been continued until the next month. He also added the defendant had told him the landowner was going to come and testify on his behalf but would not be able to come until the next month. This really took me by surprise. I thought I knew the landowner well, and this sure didn't sound right. While it wouldn't be the first time a landowner had backed up on me, I had serious doubts about it.

I thanked the judge, left the courtroom, and drove directly to the landowner's business. I walked into the business and was met by the landowner and his son. I immediately asked if they were planning to appear in court on behalf of the guys I had caught on their property. This question was met with a bewildered look and an empathic "No!" I told them the guys had asked the judge to continue the case so the landowner could come and testify on their behalf. They assured me they had no intention of coming to court unless I needed them to. I advised that would not be necessary.

A couple of days prior to court the next month, I dropped in to see the judge. I reminded him of the case and asked again why it had been continued. He again stated the defendant had asked for a continuance in order to have the landowner present. I told him I had spoken with the landowner and he assured me he had had no contact with the defendant and had no intention of being in court unless he was needed to testify against the man. The judge's aggravation was obvious.

When the judge called the cases, the defendants approached the bench. Surprisingly, they were not accompanied by their father, an attorney, the probate judge, or the landowner. The defendant pled not guilty, and the judge asked me to tell why I arrested the man. I gave the facts of the case, and the judge asked the man if the landowner was going to testify for him. The man told the judge the landowner was not able to attend. In a somewhat sarcastic tone, the judge said, "Well that's too bad." He found both the defendants guilty and gave them the maximum fine and court costs possible.

Have you ever found yourself in this type of situation? Not necessarily a hunting situation but this type of situation. These guys were guilty. They initially lied about it but eventually told the truth. When later confronted, they claimed we were in the wrong and couldn't do what we were doing. Realizing their actions had consequences, chest down on the hood of their vehicle with their hands behind their back, they decided we could do what we were doing. Again, denying the truth, they lied to the judge. However, in the end they were found guilty and paid the price.

Although they didn't want to admit it, they knew they were on the wrong side of the fence, literally and figuratively. It isn't easy admitting when we are wrong.

This is an accurate depiction of our lives. We are all sinners who have fallen short of the glory of God. In the end, our sin will be made known, and we will be found guilty of it and pay the price. The question is which side of the fence you are on. You have either admitted you are a sinner, believed Christ is God's son raised from the dead, and confessed Jesus as your Savior, or you haven't. God is clear on how he feels about those who try to straddle the fence. They make Him want to vomit. God knows which side you are on no matter what you might claim. You can't deceive Him; don't deceive yourself. If you are on the wrong side of the fence, now is the time to climb over.

Shots Fired in the Neighborhood

I HELD MY BREATH AND QUICKLY PRAYED the fellow would not fire a shot in the direction of the noise in the leaves—seeing how I was the source of the racket.

On November 29, 2007, I received a complaint from the Coosa County Sheriff's Office concerning night hunting on McClellan Lane in north central Coosa County approximately one mile below the Talladega County line. The information was sketchy. The dispatcher explained the caller had identified herself as Ms. Jones and stated she lived in the first trailer on the left on McClellan Lane. She stated a neighbor was shining a spotlight at night and shooting, and she could see this from her home. The lady told the dispatcher she did not want to be involved and would not provide her phone number. Although I understand people not wanting to be involved, I found it interesting she would not give her number, which left my only method of contacting her that of driving up in her yard in my green state truck. I made several attempts to find the caller's phone number but was unsuccessful.

I decided to travel to the area and see if I could locate a likely night-hunting spot. A general observation of the area revealed many dwellings grouped tightly together. This was definitely an unlikely looking spot; due to the great danger involved with someone shooting in such a congested area, I felt the dispatcher must have made a mistake when taking down the address. I drove through the area and was coming back along the road when a woman walked out and met me. I pulled over, and she asked if I was the game warden. I resisted the urge to say I had stolen the uniform and the green truck. She said the man in the trailer next door was shooting at night. The trailer she pointed out was less than fifty yards from her house and less than twenty-five yards from the paved road.

Noting the congested area, I asked, "Where?"

She said, "Right there," while pointing across the road to a small, grown-up field.

To the left and right of the small field were other dwellings, and through the woods beyond the field were another home and another county road. As I observed the situation, she added there was a pile of corn in the field as well. She went on to say the man had shot the previous night and had killed a deer a couple of nights earlier and stated they needed something done about it. I told her I planned to work it that night. I gave her my phone number and asked her to call me if she saw anything.

I traveled to the courthouse and had the county mapper print me a map and an aerial photo of the property. This revealed things were even more dangerous than I had first thought, with several dwellings in the possible line of fire. I had obtained the license number on a car in the driveway of the suspect residence and had the dispatcher check the registration, which provided the name of a possible suspect.

When my attempts to contact the two conservation officers in the county were unsuccessful, I contacted Talladega County CEO Jerry Fincher and told him what had transpired. He agreed to assist me with the complaint, and we made plans on how best to work it. In the meanwhile, the neighbor who had provided the info contacted me, saying she had talked with some neighbors, and I could sit in their driveways or yards or whatever I needed to do. Knowing she was only trying to help, I didn't say anything about keeping things quiet. Unfortunately, attempts to apprehend a violator are normally hampered at best and often doomed when the word gets out to the neighbors. I asked her what time the shining was taking place, and she said from 7:00 to 10:00 p.m. I thanked her for the assistance.

I met Jerry, and we traveled to the area and set up surveillance. The location of our observation point required we drive directly in front of the suspect's house. Although I would normally always avoid doing this, I didn't feel I had much choice. In addition, I felt we would be able to pull it off since my vehicle was not a typical game warden pickup but an SUV. I had phoned the informant and told her we were there and if she saw anything to give me a call.

We had been in the area for approximately an hour when we observed a vehicle pulling into the driveway of the suspect's house. Eventually I saw what appeared to be a flashlight in the yard. Shortly thereafter, the informant called and stated the suspect was shining the field with a spotlight. We moved from our vehicle into the county road but still could not observe the subject or the light. We realized we were going to have to be closer to the residence. This was disturbing in that it would require us to once again drive past the residence without being detected. We made the decision we would drive back past and out of sight of the trailer. I would then sneak back toward the residence on foot and find a position that would allow me to see what was happening. I had some night vision optics I hoped would facilitate this.

We drove past the trailer and out of sight. I pulled to the side of the road and exited the vehicle. Jerry drove to a nearby hiding spot while I made my way through the dark back toward the shooter's residence. I took up a position beside a large tree, and, as a safety precaution, I called the informant and informed her I was standing in her front yard.

Just as I was attempting to focus the night vision equipment, an occupant of the trailer turned on a light that shone out the end of the trailer. If you've ever used any night vision, you know it is for seeing in the dark, and the presence of a light can render it useless. Such was the case. Soon, with no warning whatsoever, the beam of a spotlight shone from the porch and scanned the small field across the road from the residence. My vantage point was only forty to fifty yards from the suspect. He finished shining and went back in his house. I continued to watch, and he repeated the scenario again. I could not see a firearm in his possession. I radioed Jerry and told him I felt we needed to put a stop to this whether we could arrest the man or not. A few minutes later, the suspect once again shined the field. A couple of minutes later, a man exited the rear of the trailer and smoked a cigarette.

Minutes later, the spotlight once again came on. I decided it was time to do something. Each time the man had come out on the porch, he had used the same technique. He would turn on the light and scan the field in front of his house. Then he would walk to the other end of his porch and again shine the area. I had spotted a large oak tree approximately twenty-five yards from the front porch of the house. I estimated the tree was twenty-five yards from my current position. When the man moved to the far end of the porch, I decided it was time to make my move. Unfortunately, I did not know the driveway I would be crossing en route to the tree had utility poles lying on each side of it. As I scampered toward the tree, my quiet approach immediately turned into a loud, leaf-crunching romp. As I fought to regain my balance, I could not help but notice that my thrashing through the dry leaves probably sounded a lot like a deer running. As I tried to get to the safety of the tree, I waited for the beam of the light to swing onto my position. Luckily, that didn't happen.

As I reached the tree, I quickly caught my breath and turned on my flashlight, illuminating the porch. There I observed not one but two men. I immediately yelled "state game warden" and ordered the men to raise their hands. In unison, both men bent over, which effectively took them out of my sight. I again yelled, "Put your hands up!" The men stood up with their hands over their heads. I ordered them to step off the porch and keep their hands up. I radioed Jerry and told him to come to my location. I told the men to put their hands on a vehicle in the yard, and I handcuffed them as Jerry pulled up.

With the suspects in custody, I shined my light onto the porch and there observed a high-powered rifle and a handheld spotlight. I advised the two they were under arrest. I called Coosa County Deputy Eddie Burke and asked him to come and assist us.

We separated the two suspects (a father and son) who we learned were Greg, thirty, and Leon Watson, fifty-two. They were advised of their rights and questioned. They admitted they were attempting to shoot deer and they had previously killed one deer and missed another one. Upon questioning, the son admitted he had placed corn in the field to attract deer and hunt over. The father stated he had no knowledge of the corn in the field. The dad had been shining the light, and the son was carrying the gun and planning to shoot.

Greg was arrested for hunting at night, hunting across a public road, and hunting by the aid of bait. Leon was arrested for hunting at night and hunting across a public road. Their Remington 7mm magnum rifle and a two-million-candlepower spotlight were confiscated.

When I observed the location in this story, my first thought was this couldn't be the place. Have you ever felt that way? Have you said to yourself surely you aren't in the situation you find yourself in? We must accept our situation for what it is.

After observing the violators' actions, I made the decision to move in on them. Little did I know there was literally a stumbling block in my path. Fortunately, by the grace of God, I overcame the obstacles and lived to tell the story. I hate to break it to you, but the path ahead may get rough, and you'll likely stumble. Jesus will walk it with you, if you invite Him to. The choice is yours. Choose wisely.

Joint Venture

EVIDENTLY VIOLATING WILDLIFE LAWS and regulations is just more fun when shared with family and friends. Although some violators are loners, the norm is to catch them in pairs and sometimes groups of three or four or more. Many times, violators who were members of a group felt this collaboration provided them protection from the law since it was often difficult for us to ascertain with surety who had done what. Depending on the local judge and/or DA and their knowledge of conservation violations, it could be a problem. I was very fortunate that, in my home county, our judge was very familiar with conservation law violations and was more than ready to educate and adjudicate violators.

While working a management area hunt, I received a radio call from the SO stating they needed a game warden at Billy Black's house. Billy Black was more than a familiar name to all enforcement officers in the county. Billy was known for hunting from the road, hunting at night, and many other exploits. Seeing how we were on the far side of the county with a fairly long response time, I asked the dispatcher for the nature of the problem. They stated someone had shot from the road by his house, and he was out looking for them. I knew the call was legitimate since Billy knew what a law violator looked like. He surely looked in the mirror every once in a while. It was interesting how some of our worst violators were some of the most irate complainants when their ox was being gored! I informed them we were headed toward the location.

While en route, I was relieved to hear a deputy was responding to the scene as well. Seriously, I didn't know what might occur if Billy found the subject on his property. When we arrived, I saw Billy, the deputy, and someone I assumed to be the suspect standing beside a rusted 1956 Ford pickup, one of the many ornaments in Billy's yard. Because Billy was a shade-tree mechanic, many of the hopeless cases evidently found their final resting place on the property—at least until the price of scrap metal went up again.

Shortly after my arrival, the local game warden arrived, and we began gathering details. Our culprit, or suspect, as the news today calls someone who has been caught red handed committing a crime, was in his thirties, of medium build, with a ruddy complexion. He wore blue jeans, a plaid flannel shirt, and a light jacket. I surmised these were his riding-around-shooting-out-the-window clothes and not his normal hunting clothes—unless, of course, that was the way he normally hunted! He was not in possession of a firearm but did possess a knife. It was interesting how more often than not when we asked someone if they had any weapons, they never considered a knife to be a weapon. We did. Had it been early in the fall, I would have thought the fellow had bitten hard into a green persimmon, judging by the look on his face.

Leaving the suspect with the deputy, we took Billy to the side and asked him what had occurred. He stated a vehicle had passed slowly by his house, and he had heard a shot. He observed a subject exiting the vehicle and going into the woods while two other individuals in the truck left the scene. Billy went into the woods and found the man, who was retrieving a freshly killed illegal button buck. With this information in hand, we then questioned the suspect.

Let me pause here to enlighten you concerning a biological fact I learned through observation. Evidently wildlife violations are very often closely correlated with the need to use the bathroom. Wildlife law violators are a very discreet group in that they do not use the bathroom just anywhere; they want to get well off the road, where deer are known to frequent, to handle such matters. This must be true since this was this guy's story as well. It seems his buddies had let him out of the truck to go into the woods and use the bathroom. Obviously, someone using the bathroom was embarrassing to them, as they had to drive away and come back and pick him up later. Unfortunately, he had picked a location where someone else had just (literally seconds earlier) shot an illegal deer. Evidently seeing Billy standing on the side of the road with their "bathroom using" friend when they returned for him was more than his buddies could bear. They were so embarrassed they simply drove on past and did not come back. Oh, the shame!

After listening to this pitiful story, I tried to show compassion when I told him his story didn't make a lick of sense. I tried to tactfully worm the truth out of the guy, but he wouldn't give it up. Our seasoned game warden decided to take over the questioning. Now his style was a bit different from mine. It wasn't really questioning at all. Basically, he would tell the suspect what he felt had happened and would browbeat them into agreeing with his assessment. Amazingly, the suspect would often admit their guilt! In this case, the officer was getting more and more aggravated with the suspect and finally yelled at the guy, "Who shot that deer?" I thought to myself this type of heavy-handed badgering of the man wasn't going to get us anywhere. Of course, just as I thought that, the suspect yelled back, "I shot it!" With this heartfelt admission, we loaded the man in the truck and took him to jail.

We actually did not place the man in jail, but we also did not want to leave him there with Billy. At the jail, we wrote tickets for hunting without a permit, hunting from the public road, hunting by aid of a vehicle, and taking an illegal deer. We questioned him thoroughly and received the names and addresses of his accomplices. With all the paperwork complete, we told the subject he could phone someone to come and pick him up. He went to the phone and called someone telling them he needed to be picked up at the jail. He paused and looked at us and asked if we would arrest his buddies if they came to get him. We told him that was a good possibility. It was almost comical when he told them our answer and then pleaded, "Y'all, somebody needs to come get me!" We waited around just in case but weren't surprised when a female arrived to pick him up.

After consulting with Billy and learning he could identify the other subjects, we obtained warrants for their arrest on the same charges. Having to obtain the warrants and having to locate the individuals created a situation where the defendant's court appearances were set for two consecutive court dates. This set the stage for an interesting courtroom experience.

When his name was called, Jimmy, the first caught, dejectedly approached the judge's bench. The judge read off the charges, and Jimmy promptly pled guilty. The judge accepted his plea and levied fines and court costs in the amount of $1,535. The sentence for each charge also carried thirty days in jail. The judge explained he would suspend the jail time if the fines and court costs were paid in full. He then asked his patented question, "Are you going to pay it or sit it out?" The defendant quickly stated he had the money with him. I think his brief time spent at the jail had shown him he did not want to be in the jail.

JOINT VENTURE

The next month, the two accomplices were in court and approached the bench when their names were called. Both fellows were gray headed and appeared to be in their late fifties or early sixties, much older than their codefendant. The judge advised the duo they were charged with hunting from the road, from the vehicle, without a permit, and taking an illegal deer. He asked, "How do you plead?" One of the two stepped forward and proudly announced their friend Jimmy had been in court the previous month and had pled guilty to the charges and had already paid the fine. Obviously, the defendant felt this information would absolve him of any responsibility in this endeavor. However, he was about to receive a bit of wisdom from the judge that I have used many times since and don't think I will ever forget.

The judge looked at the man and asked, "Sir, are you familiar with the term *joint venture*?" With a puzzled look on his face, the fellow replied he didn't think he was. The always-helpful judge told the man a joint venture was when two or three people got together and did something and the outcome of what they did affected the whole group. The man still looked a bit confused when the judge announced, "Sir, you were on a joint venture!"

I could tell by the judge's increased breathing rate and slightly clenched teeth this was not going to go well for this duo. My inclination was on target, and without me giving a word of testimony, the judge threw the book at the two, levying fines and costs of $2,200 each! While the pair stood in shock, the judge again posed his routine question, "Are you going to pay it or sit it out?" I'm not sure the fellows understood this meant you could pay the fines and be on your way, or you could start doing the jail time he had linked to the sentence. However, after thinking for a few seconds, the spokesman for the pair said he guessed he could mortgage his house and come up with the money. To that the judge responded, "Whatever it takes. Until then you are in the custody of the sheriff." The shell-shocked men were escorted to seats with the rest of the criminals.

A couple of months later, I met the judge in the hallway of the courthouse, and he called me aside and told me he had reduced a fine that morning. He asked if I remembered the two guys we had caught hunting from the road, and I assured him I did. He said the two road hunters had come in with $4,304 of the $4,400 needed to settle their case. Being in the Christmas spirit, he had graciously reduced the fine by $96 so they could satisfy the obligation. I told him he was all heart. To the best of my knowledge, I never saw any of those individuals again. I don't know, but I think it would be a safe bet they did their best to avoid any more "joint ventures!"

The Bible says bad company corrupts good morals. As I prepared to leave home headed to graduate school in Starkville, Mississippi, my daddy gave me some sage advice. He said there are good people everywhere, and it was my job to find them. Working enforcement for over thirty years, I have witnessed many folks who were led down a bad path. Although you may get caught up and go along with the crowd, remember that everyone will be held individually accountable. If you want to take part in a joint venture, join up with Jesus!

Apples Don't Fall Far

"THEY'RE NOT GOING TO MAKE IT," I yelled as the car began fishtailing while approaching the narrow bridge. The paved county road was as crooked as a dog's hind leg and was not built for high speeds. Miraculously, the driver held the car in the road, and soon we were once again nearing one hundred miles per hour. It was by far the longest and fastest chase I had ever been in, and it was about to come to a quick end.

During the 1990s, night hunting of deer was rampant in Coosa County, Alabama. At the time, our rural county was the northernmost county in the state with a high whitetail deer population. Therefore, we were a mecca for night hunters from northern counties that had few if any deer and for those homegrown outlaws as well. This was true despite the fact my partners and I caught many night hunters each year and our district court judge consistently hammered them. Our judge was conservation minded and held a special disdain for those who would molest our natural resources. Unlike many judges, he understood night hunting was a serious crime—not only because of the damage done to the resource but also because anyone unleashing a projectile traveling at three thousand feet per second into the dark of night with no idea or concern where it would end up was beyond reckless and deserved a severe reprimand. Night hunters were generally charged with hunting at night, hunting from a public road, and hunting by the aid of a vehicle. At the time, the minimum fines and court costs for these charges would total over $800. In addition, any item used in the commission of the crime, including firearms and vehicles, was subject to being confiscated. Still, the night hunting was widespread, and it seemed the only light at the end of a tunnel was a Q-Beam spotlight.

Saturday night found both county game wardens and me with our deer decoy set up on Coosa County Road 40, a favorite night hunting hot spot. Although illegal activity occurred every night of the week, the weekend normally was the most active. Some folks did not have to work on the weekend, and others only came into the county on the weekend. We stood outside our vehicles in the crisp winter air under a clear sky. Standing outside under these conditions allowed us to hear a shot for a distance of a mile or more. County Road 40 led to several hunting camps. This combined with our mounted deer set up along the road would hopefully bring us, the violators, and their quarry all together at the same time and place.

Traffic had been relatively light when a Dodge K-car eased to a stop parallel to the mounted deer. Soon the quiet evening was shattered by the py-yow of a high-powered rifle. Before we could even move, the passenger shot for the second time. Without a flinch from the fake deer, the driver realized things weren't kosher, and he mashed the gas pedal to the floor.

County Road 40 wasn't the best or the straightest road in the county. As a matter of fact, it appeared to have been engineered by a drunk following a snake. I knew a high-speed chase on this road would be a real adventure, and I was about to find that out firsthand.

Within seconds after the shots, we were flying down the road in hot pursuit of the violator's vehicle. The Coosa County game warden, Hershel Patterson, was immediately behind the subjects in his Ford Crown Victoria, and his partner, Earl Brown, and I were right behind him in Earl's four-wheel-drive pickup. I had been in a few brief chases during my short career, and it looked as though we were in another, as these individuals did not appear to have any inclination to pull over. Knowing the road as I did, I felt certain if they didn't slow down soon, the curves and the narrow bridge they were fast approaching would probably terminate the chase.

As we headed down the hill toward Jack's Creek, a quick glance at the speedometer showed we were running just less than one hundred miles per hour. "He'll never make the bridge," I yelled. It's interesting how your voice seems to go up in pitch during times of stress. As the defendants neared the narrow bridge, I saw the taillights of the car begin to sway from side to side. Anticipating a crash, we all backed off. Miraculously the driver made it across the bridge; however, he did lose much of his momentum. This allowed us to once again close the gap. At this point, Earl began to formulate a plan to end the pursuit. He told me when we reached the straight stretch of road just ahead, we were going to pass both Hershel and the suspects and slide sideways in front of their car. I must admit I had some reservations about this plan. However, seeing how I was in the passenger's seat, I didn't really have a lot of control over the situation. About the time I asked, "Don't we need to tell Hershel the plan?" Earl slammed the accelerator to the floor, and I became very busy just hanging on.

Speeds were back up near a hundred as we pulled out and began passing the two vehicles. Realizing we would soon be sliding in front of the armed suspects, I asked Earl where his shotgun was. He told me it was under the seat. I quickly learned you should always have your shotgun easily accessible to you. Try as I might, I could not get the gun out from under the seat. It was not lost on me that the upcoming maneuver would put me directly in front of a pair of fleeing criminals armed with a high-powered rifle!

Earl was a master mechanic prior to becoming a conservation officer, so his truck was far from your standard low-bid state vehicle. The 351-cubic-inch engine with the four-barrel carburetor packed a little more punch than the suspects' compact car could muster and we were soon past the car and were preparing to slide sideways in front of them.

All of this was new to me and was blowing my mind. The chase had now gone about seven miles at speeds of one hundred miles per hour. Thankfully, we did not meet another vehicle during the entire chase. It was a wild ride, but it was about to come to an abrupt halt.

I had my hand on the barrel of the shotgun, and as we slid to a stop, I threw open my door and snatched the shotgun from under the seat. The vehicle literally slid to within a few feet of me, and I was soon lying prone on their hood with the Remington 870 shotgun pointed at the driver's face. I knew the shotgun did not have a shell in the chamber; however, the subjects didn't have the luxury of that knowledge. I yelled at the driver to turn the car off and raise his hands over his head. Looking down the business end of a 12-gauge shotgun, which I'm sure looked as big as a trash can when it was three feet from his face, the driver complied. Hershel was soon at the passenger's door, snatching the passenger and his 30-06 rifle out of the car. Earl opened the driver's door and brought him around and placed him on the hood. Hershel laid the passenger across the hood as well, and it quickly became obvious to everyone in the vicinity "the smell of fear" was emanating from the man's pants. While being patted down, the suspect stated he needed to use the bathroom, and Hershel replied, "I think it's a little late for that!" The Rockford police had been monitoring the chase on the radio and had come to assist us. Since it was the only vehicle with a cage in the back, we placed both subjects in the Rockford patrol car and Chief Mike Arms transported the smelly duo to the county jail.

At the jail, the pair were allowed to make a call for someone to come and bond them out. They were placed in a cell while we completed the mountain of paperwork that accompanied arrests of this type. Within about an hour, the driver's wife arrived at the jail to pick up the two subjects. We had decided to allow them to sign their own bonds for hunting at night, hunting without a permit, hunting from the road, and hunting by aid of a vehicle and then to bond out through the jail on the attempting-to-elude charge.

The defendants were probably pretty tired of signing documents; however, one of them wasn't quite finished yet. When he was brought out of his cell and into the lobby area of the jail, he was met by his wife, who demanded he hand over his hunting license. Although his first response was to dismiss the demand, it was soon made clear if he wanted to leave the jail with her, he would comply with her wishes. After handing over his license, his wife presented the defendant with a handwritten agreement and told him to sign it. Although I couldn't see the entire document, I saw enough to realize it was a full-page list of dos and don'ts: I will replace the front screen door, I will not hunt with Terry Brody, I will not hunt illegally, and so forth. "Sign it," she said in a tone that meant business. The man briefly looked at the list and disgustedly signed it.

The cases came to court the next month. The defendants pled guilty to all of the charges and paid fines and court costs totaling over $2,500. The passenger's Remington 30-06 rifle was forfeited, and both subjects' hunting privileges were revoked for a period of three years. Each individual also received thirty days of jail time that was suspended on the payment of the fines and court costs.

Approximately ten years later, things had changed significantly. Night hunting for deer was still prevalent; however, I found myself working it by myself most of the time. After nearly thirty years as a game warden, Hershel retired. We had worked closely together for the last few years, and I was quickly realizing how much I had relied on his input and guidance. While I regularly worked on my own, having a partner had been a tremendous asset. Hershel never came out and worked with me after his retirement; however, we did talk on a regular basis, and he continued to be a great source of information.

As the rain was pounding on my roof one cool winter night, my phone rang. I answered the call and recognized Hershel's voice on the line. He stated someone had just shot in his stepdaughter's yard, which was adjacent to his yard. I told him I was on the way.

Many folks hear about someone night hunting and automatically assume the activity is taking place in some remote area away from main roads and houses. While night hunting occurs in those places, it also happens along US highways and in people's front yards. In this situation, the deer were standing between the shooters and Hershel's stepdaughter's home. Believe me when I tell you this type scenario was not at all unusual. I once placed the deer decoy within fifty yards of the corner of a house with a car in the driveway, and the first vehicle that passed by stopped, and the driver shot the deer. Although no one lived in the house, the shooter did not know that and evidently did not care!

About two minutes after receiving Hershel's call I was in my truck and en route. The pouring rain slowed my progress. On a good, clear night with little traffic, I could make it to Hershel's house within about fifteen minutes. That's normally much longer than a night hunter would remain on the scene. My windshield wipers were beating out a relentless rhythm as I pushed as hard as I could. Fortunately, the torrent eased off as I neared the location.

Arriving on the scene, I found Hershel and his wife, Mary, had the subjects detained. Hershel gave me a quick synopsis, saying the pair had pulled into his stepdaughter's driveway and shot twice. The two young men had actually killed two deer and pulled out into the field in an attempt to retrieve them. That proved to be a mistake, seeing how it gave Hershel enough time to get on the scene and use his vehicle to block the driveway, which was the only avenue of escape.

Two dour-looking chaps were standing at the front of their vehicle as I approached and requested their identification. While one subject handed me his driver's license, the other told me he did not have any identification. I asked his age and he stated he was eighteen. I advised the young man people without identification got processed through the jail and asked his name. He replied, "Matthew Johnson."

The name immediately triggered the database in my mind, and I asked, "What's your daddy's name?"

"Eddie Johnson," he answered.

"Matthew Eddie Johnson?" I asked.

There was obvious curiosity in his voice when he replied, "Yes." I turned to Hershel and said, "The apple doesn't fall far from the tree."

The young night hunter immediately asked, "What does that mean?" I told him it meant I caught his daddy doing the same thing! The boy replied, "He told me not to come to Coosa County and do this," and I responded, "Well, you should have listened to him!"

Since the truck owner did not possess any identification, the decision was made to process the pair through the jail. We retrieved the two deer and loaded them and the subjects in my vehicle and headed to the county jail. The parents were notified and soon arrived.

You never knew how parents would react to the apprehension of their little angel. Some were apologetic, some upset with their child, and some highly agitated with the lowly law enforcement officer who had the audacity to do his job and write up a kid for what they considered doing nothing more than being a kid! The fact they had just taken the life of an animal by firing a shot in the dark of night directly at an occupied house was simply beside the point! Fortunately, these parents didn't have a lot to say.

The pair were arrested for taking deer at night, hunting from a public road, hunting without a permit, and hunting by the aid of a vehicle. The deer were donated to the county jail and would be processed and fed to the prisoners.

In district court, the young age of the perpetrators was taken into consideration by the judge. This did not necessarily mean the judge felt sorry for the defendants nor believed it was a youthful indiscretion. It often meant the judge sensed the parents or sometimes grandparents would be the ones footing the bill. An agreement was reached where we would drop the charges of hunting by the aid of a vehicle and hunting from a public road. The duo paid fines and court costs totaling over $1,300, and the young Johnson forfeited his Remington model 7600 rifle. Reflecting back on the case shortly after it had occurred, I told Hershel, "I guess it's a definite sign you're getting old when you start catching second-generation night hunters!"

Fifteen years after the first case in this story, I was conducting a training class for local enforcement officers. In many regards wildlife law enforcement is unlike any other type of law enforcement. Seasoned officers from police departments, sheriff's offices, and the highway patrol often were at a loss as to how to handle game and fish cases. On numerous occasions, I would conduct a class to give these officers, and new conservation officers, insight into the elements of our cases and the ploys and strategies our violators employed. During these classes I would share several stories of different cases.

During a break, Rockford Police Chief Mike Arms came up and told me the worst case he ever got into with us was the night he came to assist us at Highway 22 and County Road 40. He said, "When I pulled up, it looked like a swat team." He lamented, "That was a bad night to be the only one there with a cage in the car, I think that car still had "the smell of fear" in it when we got rid of it!" He went on to say, "You know, I should have written that stuff down, but nobody would believe it."

Well, chief, they may not believe it, but at least it's written down!

Folks, there is no doubt apples don't fall far from the tree. I once heard it said we teach what we know, but we reproduce what we are. Proverbs says raise up a child in the way they should go, and when they are old they will not depart from it. Dads, we have to do our best to train our children well. That will happen much more by what we do than by what we say. Remember, apples don't fall far.

Waiting for Daylight

CONTRARY TO THE POPULAR BELIEF of many violators, the deer decoy was not used to entrap people, it was used to reveal folks' true intentions. Everybody going through our rural county would pass by numerous deer standing alongside the road during both day and night. Only a few took the opportunity to shoot at them. The choice was theirs.

In response to complaints of people shooting before daylight I decided to set up the fake deer on the main entrance road of the wildlife management area (WMA). The decoy was a great tool for determining whether or not someone was inclined to break the law. For us, the decoy was simply a tool that allowed us to place the violator, the officer and what appeared to be a deer in the same location at the same time.

I placed the deer well off the side of the roadway leading into the WMA where it would be difficult for anyone driving normally to spot it. Evidently, I did a good job seeing how several vehicles rolled by without giving any indication they had spotted the stuffed wonder. However, eventually the driver of a slow-moving truck angled his vehicle so his headlights illuminated the decoy. With my hand on the key in the ignition I anxiously anticipated the shot I felt certain would soon split the early morning calm.

As I watched, the driver put the vehicle in reverse and began slowly backing up. I felt certain the man was maneuvering for a better shot angle however to my surprise the driver eased the truck off the side of the road and turned off the engine.

My mind was now spinning. Was this guy going to get out of the truck and stalk the deer or what? A walking night hunter was one of the most dangerous things we could encounter. With this in mind I kept my eyes peeled on the truck in front of me.

After a couple of minutes had passed with no movement I was considering what I needed to do. I didn't know what this guy was doing but I felt certain the decoy would not be effective with a pickup truck sitting across the road from it! I decided I was going to have to check this guy out and hopefully have him move on. I pulled my truck behind the parked vehicle, activated my blue lights and approached the driver's door. I illuminated the driver, the only occupant of the truck, with my flashlight. He appeared to be seriously surprised that I had driven out of the woods directly behind him. As I examined the interior of the truck I noticed the man had his rifle immediately beside him with the muzzle pointed down. I asked if the gun was loaded and he replied it was. Having a loaded firearm in a vehicle was the most common violation on the WMA. I asked the man for his license and permit and he produced both. When I asked what he was doing sitting on the side of the road, he replied he had spotted a buck on the opposite side of the road and was waiting on it to get light enough that he could shoot it. "From the truck?" I asked and he sheepishly replied, "Yes."

I explained he was in violation by having his gun loaded in the vehicle, he was also hunting from the vehicle, hunting from a public road and hunting at night. As you might guess that fist full of tickets would cost a pretty penny. However since he had resisted the temptation to shoot the deer from the truck and from the road when he easily could have, I believed him when he said his intent was to wait on daylight. Therefore, I wrote him a ticket for the loaded gun. I gave him the ticket and he thanked me for being lenient with him. He went on his way and I collected the decoy and headed toward the WMA checking station. Although I had already been working for about three hours I knew it would be about twelve more before I would head for home.

What about you? This guy was waiting on the light. Jesus said He is the light of the world in Him there is no darkness. The Bible says those who walk without the light, stumble. If you are stumbling in the dark, come to the light. Choose Him today and you will never have to walk in the dark or alone again.

We Play Hardball

THE BELLY CHAINS AND LEG SHACKLES made a rhythmic cadence as the prisoner shuffled up to the judge's bench. The crowd listened with interest as the judge reminded the man why he was there.

It was very common for the general public and, unfortunately, even some of the judiciary to consider violations of game and fish laws and regulations as minor or trivial. This is somewhat understandable when we commonly, on a daily basis, are bombarded by reports of murder, robbery, burglary, and other heinous crimes. Someone fishing without a license or exceeding the bag limit on squirrels obviously doesn't compare with many other misdemeanor crimes; however, it is against the law. Part of our job was to enforce the law, and we took it seriously. Obviously, we have laws and regulations that are more significant than others and more dangerous to enforce. It is logical to assume that arresting someone for hunting at night, which carries a minimum $2,000 fine, would present more danger than arresting someone fishing without a license. That being said we have had more than one officer who ended up in a deadly force situation resulting from an attempt to check the license of a fisherman.

Law enforcement officers never know what an encounter will lead to. There is no such thing as a routine stop or call. Many officers have died attempting to apprehend a violator they had dealt with many times before without incident.

In the courtroom of a rural county where hunting and fishing opportunities abound and an active officer resides, the court docket will often hold many game and fish cases. Early in my career when the two game wardens in the county and I were working seventy hours a week, our hunting season court dockets would often be predominately made up of hunting cases. In a court like ours, the judge often took a dim view of game and fish law violators, while in jurisdictions with few game and fish cases, the judges often viewed the cases as a waste of time. There were many variables involved in this, but that's another entire story.

The Coosa County courtroom was on the second floor of the courthouse, which sat at the intersection of US Highway 231 and Alabama Highway 22 and was by far the largest building in the county seat of Rockford. The layout was much like most courtrooms I had seen. The judge's bench was elevated front and center of the large room. On the left of the judge was the witness stand, and the right side was occupied by the court clerk, who recorded all the proceedings. To the far left was an elevated box that held a dozen wooden chairs for jurors. In front of the bench were two large tables. The state prosecutor normally sat at the table on the left, and defense attorneys sat on the right. This setup allowed us to say the defense attorneys were on the right side. You normally couldn't say that! Along the right wall were chairs where the officers who had cases coming up would sit. In front of the judge was a large gallery that would seat approximately three hundred people.

For the first twenty-five years of my career, it was common practice for the jailers to bring prisoners from the jail and have them sit in the jury box while waiting to have their case called.

After our county experienced a courtroom shooting (another story), security was tightened significantly.

During 2011, I witnessed an event in district court that got the attention of all of those in attendance. At precisely 9:00 a.m., Coosa County Sheriff's Sgt. Eddie Burke summoned all to rise as Judge Carlton Teel entered the courtroom and took his place on the bench. Every eye was on the judge as he announced court was in session.

"When your name is called, approach the bench" was his instruction to those present. He called the first name on the docket, and a small young man stood up in the jury box and began to make his way to the bench. This wasn't easy seeing how the man, dressed in an orange jumpsuit, was wearing a belly chain attached to handcuffs and leg shackles. It took almost a minute for the man to shuffle the thirty feet to the judge's bench. From his lofty perch the fierce eagle glared at the cowering starling and announced, "Sir, you have been charged with fishing without a license. How do you plead?" There was a hushed but audible gasp in the courtroom.

There were several officers in the courtroom and the majority of them were standing with me on the south side of the room. Standing beside me was an alcoholic beverage control agent from a neighboring county who wasn't familiar with our court. Noting the surprised look on his face, I leaned over to him and whispered, "We play hardball up here."

He replied, "I'm going to get me some license soon as we get out of here!"

Even the judge appeared to be taken aback when he heard what the man was charged with. He asked the man if he had been arrested for failure to appear, and the man nodded yes, thereby clarifying why he was trussed up. The judge inquired as to how long the man had been in jail, and he replied thirty days. The judge advised the man he would be released on time served. Although when speaking with the other officer I was referring to the felony wardrobe the man was wearing, I would say thirty days in jail for fishing without a twelve-dollar license was playing hard ball.

What about you? Have you ever played hardball? When we use that phrase, we are often indicating that no punches are pulled and you play all out. Folks, that's the way life is. Life rarely pulls any punches. We are often hit right in the gut, and sometimes while we are bowed over we catch it right in the back of the head. We often use the adage "When it rains, it pours," indicating that life keeps throwing things our way. Life is too hard to go it alone. Luckily, we don't have to. The Bible tells us we can lay our burdens at the feet of the Savior. While He doesn't take away our trials and tribulations, He does walk with us through them. Believe me when I tell you, it makes all the difference. He is waiting on you to call out to Him. Do it now; there's likely another hard ball coming your way.

It Was My Crossbow!

MANY PEOPLE QUESTION THE ACTIONS of law enforcement officers because they are under the misconception that people encountered by law enforcement act rationally. You should never assume that.

Something I always tried to point out to people who were interested in a job like mine was the fact that when everyone else was hunting, we were working. This was especially true during the holidays. The week from Christmas to New Year's was always active with several violations taking place. While most people were enjoying some time off work with their families and hunting, we were usually busy working. It was one of the sacrifices officers were forced to make. The increased activity, both day and night, often prompted us to work pretty much around the clock. On more than one occasion, we apprehended night hunters on Christmas night and confiscated the rifle that had been under the Christmas tree only hours earlier. Believe me when I tell you that would often bring a violator to tears.

While working a perpetual night hunting hot spot, Wildlife and Freshwater Fisheries Division Sgt. Matt Weathers (now chief of enforcement) experienced what would hopefully be a once-in-a-lifetime event. Watching a large green field from a good honey hole, Matt observed a Dodge Dakota pickup, much like the state-issued vehicle he was sitting in, make its way slowly down the road. It was Christmas night.

It was a good night for night hunting, cold and crisp. The small pickup eased along the road, and soon the field was illuminated with a spotlight. Matt watched as the poacher "worked" the field with the light. Easing out of his hiding place, he approached the truck. He activated his blue lights, and the driver immediately pulled to the side of the road.

Approaching someone who is most likely armed and who has just broken several laws that will likely cost them thousands of dollars and possibly the loss of their firearm and vehicle is not a situation relished by many. This is one of the most dangerous times for an officer, and you can be assured they are on high alert. In my opinion, there are probably few officers better prepared for this type situation than the one in this story. Matt is a well-rounded tactics and firearms instructor. He always took training seriously and is an excellent trainer. I always appreciated his attention to detail and willingness to work with all of us to get it right.

The sergeant exited his truck and started toward the stationary vehicle. Seeing the driver's window was down, the officer gave the loud verbal command for the driver to raise his hands. However, instead of seeing the driver's hands come out the window, the rear window of the truck exploded sending shards of glass into the air and the approaching officer scampering for cover. He moved across the road and achieved a safe tactical position. During this time the driver, the sole occupant of the truck, was hollering at the top of his lungs. Although still startled, the officer finally figured out the fellow was yelling, "It's my crossbow! It's my crossbow!" Matt assessed the situation and, giving loud verbal commands, moved toward the driver. He removed the man from the vehicle and secured him. The whole time the man was trying to explain what had happened. With everything secure, Matt was able to listen to the violator's explanation.

While I have heard several accounts of how a rifle or shotgun discharged while a violator was attempting to unload or hide it, this was a first. As you can imagine the officer was interested in finding out just what had occurred. The man explained to Matt he did not want to have a loaded crossbow for Matt to find when he approached the vehicle, so he pointed the weapon into the front floorboard and pulled the trigger. The broadhead tipped bolt hit the floorboard and careened wildly through the vehicle before exiting through the back glass! Remember what I said about folks not being rational.

While the story was almost unbelievable, it wasn't the end of the story. The fellow went on to explain the reason he was hunting with the crossbow. Pointing across the field to a farmhouse in the distance he proclaimed, "I was night hunting here last year and the guy in that house shot at me, so I got a crossbow so he couldn't hear me shoot." Even with that great justification, the violator was arrested for hunting at night, hunting from a public road, and hunting without a permit. You can't make this stuff up.

The outlaw in this story was like many of us in that he did not change his bad behavior; he simply attempted to modify it so he could get by without a consequence. What about you? Has the Lord been telling you to turn from your wicked ways and you've only turned enough that maybe He can't see as well? That will not cut it. He says to turn from your wicked ways, humble yourself and pray. It's the only real solution. The guy with the crossbow was lucky he survived his bonehead actions. Have you ever done anything stupid? Today you can make it right. Do it now before it is everlastingly too late.

Thank Goodness It's the Game Warden

AS ODD AS IT MAY SOUND, deciding when to call it a night and head for home when trying to apprehend those who try to illegally kill deer at night is often difficult for a conservation enforcement officer (CEO). One might think after an officer has sat in the middle of nowhere for hours in the pitch-black dark without seeing or even hearing a vehicle they would be ready to go home. The problem is the rule. Any CEO who has worked a season or two knows the rule. The rule says after sitting on a stake out for hours with no activity, you will meet a highly suspect vehicle as soon as you leave your hiding spot. I'm telling you it is uncanny how often this happens. Many officers follow another rule which is the fifteen-minute rule. That rule says when you have stayed as long as you can, wait fifteen more minutes. It sometimes makes the difference.

After working a long night, the CEO had just slipped into bed when the phone rang. The clock read 2:03 a.m. He could not believe he had just sat in the cold dark night for over six hours without seeing anyone and now he was about to receive a complaint. He answered the phone and the excited fellow on the other end of the line told him "they" had caught some night hunters and needed him to come right away. The caller said they were near the big tree just past the crossroads. I guess every town or community has a landmark that everyone recognizes even when it is no longer there. It might be a long-horned cow, the site of an old mill or in our case in Coosa County it was the big oak in Kellyton. Even after the tree was cut down and removed, the location was still known as the big oak in Kellyton. It still is today.

The officer told the caller it would take at least an hour for him to reach them and the man replied that was okay, "they had them." The officer got his uniform and gun belt on and headed toward the location. One of the most potentially volatile situations you could have was when a landowner apprehended a violator. Some folks handled things just right while others tended to lose their heads.

After a quick forty-five-minute drive, the officer arrived on the scene and was somewhat shocked by what he observed. A small car was boxed in with a pickup in front and behind it. There were two men laying spread eagle in the road while a third man stood over them pointing a shotgun at one and then the other. A fourth man seemed to be supervising the "guard." As the officer exited his truck the supervisor ran to him and told him the two men on the ground were night hunters. The officer approached the men and told the gunman he could put his gun away. He told the violators they could get up off the cold asphalt. The temperature was maybe twenty-five degrees and neither man was wearing a heavy coat. Their shivering was evident and he told them to have a seat in his truck. He briefly talked with the fellow who had been holding them, a local hunting club member. The man explained the pair had slowly eased along the road shining a spotlight out the window. He had jumped in his truck and pursued them. He passed them and slid his truck sideways in the road making them stop. His brother-in-law had pulled in behind them blocking any path of escape. They had taken the men out of their vehicle at gun point and had told them to "assume the position" face down in the road. He added, "there's a gun in their car too."

While there were several things the officer needed to address with the club members, he decided to return to the prisoners and hear what they had to say. The first thing the men said was they had never been so happy to see the game warden. They told him they had been held at gunpoint on the ground for what seemed like two hours. The pair admitted they had been night hunting and would gladly confess as long as they would not be turned back over to the vigilantes. The officer took their confessions and escorted the pair back to their vehicle. He said he had never been thanked so profusely by a night hunter.

The officer took the opportunity to explain to the two "captors" the many things that could have gone horribly wrong when they were attempting to apprehend two armed violators. He emphasized their lack of authority and how things could have gone south so quickly. The men stated they understood. He gave them the court date and sent them on their way.

In my experience, it was extremely rare indeed that we arrived on a night hunting scene and the night hunters wanted to hug our neck! What about you? When your time is up will it be joy or gloom. That decision is yours today.

Don't Touch It

WITH MY PARTNER STANDING out by the road, the vehicle came easing back along the highway. The car rolled to a stop, and a shot rang out. The vehicle immediately took off. "They've shot Byron" was the first thing that went through my mind. I started the truck and tore out toward the road, hoping I was wrong.

Night hunting was running rampant in Coosa County. The numerous deer standing along the side of the road each night were more temptation than many folks could stand. It seemed like we were getting a complaint every night. I had called CEO Byron Smith in neighboring Elmore County and asked if he could give us some assistance. He agreed, and we set the time for him to meet at my house.

I had the decoy loaded and waiting when Byron arrived. We got in my truck and made the short trip to where we were going to set up. When I say short trip, it was literally less than a half mile from the end of my driveway. My nearest neighbors, Randy and Annette Spivey, had contacted me on several occasions, reporting spotlighting and shooting in front of their home on Alabama Highway 22. I had decided to set the decoy up on the edge of their property in hopes our shooters would try it again. The setup had to be just right since, if the deer was visible from the wrong angle, a shot could go right through the Spiveys' house. As bad as they wanted them caught, they didn't want to be shot! I had responded to numerous houses being shot into in the past, one just down the road from this one, so I definitely didn't want to add to that problem.

Byron was the decoy guru. He started building and using decoys years earlier and knew all the tricks of the trade. I consider myself fortunate to have received training from him. He actually made all the decoys we used. Soon after this incident, he retired and developed a very successful decoy business.

With the decoy set, we backed up the driveway of an abandoned farmhouse across the road. A couple of hours into our vigil, a car passed the deer, and we noticed they decelerated. The more experienced road hunters would not slam on their brakes but would simply ease off the gas. The vehicle proceeded down the road but quickly returned and again eased past the deer. I was happy to see they drove past since this was the direction I definitely didn't want them to shoot from. It was not unusual for a vehicle to make a couple of passes before shooting the decoy, so we sat tight. Sure enough, the vehicle came back and made another pass and another and another. Byron said he could not understand what was going on and decided to go down to the road and see if he could determine what the people were doing and why they weren't shooting the deer. Although we didn't think the vehicle had stopped, it would not be the first time we had been forced to run people off who, thinking the deer was real, would blow their horn or get out and shout at the manikin.

Byron hurried down to the road, and, sure enough, the vehicle came back for its sixth pass. Just as the car reached the decoy, a shot split the night. My heart jumped into my throat as my first thought was, "They've shot Byron!" I cranked the truck and nearly yanked the gearshift off. I raced to the road, and thank goodness

Byron ran up and jumped in the truck. I tore out toward Rockford, the county seat of our rural county, in pursuit of the violators. As I topped a rise in the road, just above my driveway, the suspects' vehicle had stopped in the road ahead; however, seeing my headlights, the driver took off in a cloud of smoke. I never liked high-speed chases. Not that I didn't enjoy the chase, I was afraid my low-bid pickup would not be able to keep up with the vehicle I was pursuing. Fortunately, the vehicle I was pursuing this night, a small four-door sedan, wasn't just off the lot, and I was able to close the distance between us fairly quickly.

As we neared the only stop sign in the center of the county seat, I was running about eighty miles per hour. However, only a quarter mile from the four-way stop, the vehicle dipped off on a side street. Although I didn't know it, I was about to learn a lesson about antilock brakes. As the car veered left down the side street, I realized I had up a little too much speed to follow. I got on the brakes hard, and, just when I felt I had slowed enough to make the turn, the antilock released and the truck accelerated again. With both hands on the steering wheel and a firm attachment to the vinyl seat, I somehow negotiated the turn and stayed behind the vehicle. Realizing the turn didn't shake us off their tail, the outlaw decided to jam on their brakes and slid to a stop. Thinking I was going to knock them on down the road, I once again applied the brakes and thankfully stopped within inches of their bumper.

I immediately exited the truck and approached the car. I noted there were two children in the back seat and two men in the front. I was yelling for everyone to raise their hands while looking for a firearm. The occupants did raise their hands, yet I did not see a rifle. However, I did see the butt of a revolver sticking out from between the front seats. Just as I saw the gun, the driver did something I will never understand or forget. With his right hand, he reached down and grasped the grip of the pistol. Placing my

.357 revolver six inches from his left ear, I yelled at the top of my lungs, "Don't touch it!"

You may have heard about or experienced the phenomenon of having everything seem to go into slow motion. The first time I ever remember this happening was when I was sixteen years old and my neighbor and I were tumbling end over end in his four-wheel-drive pickup. I remember seeing the windshield coming toward me and putting up my arm so my elbow could smash through it. We had survived that one relatively unharmed; however, I was once again having a slow-motion experience, and this time there was a loaded gun in my hand pointed at a man's head. Although I was fixated on the gun in the man's hand, my thoughts were on something else. I was thinking I was about to literally blow this man's head off, right in front of his kids. That thought was what kept me from squeezing the trigger as the man started up with the pistol. As my finger tightened on the trigger, I yelled again, and the man let go of the gun and raised his hand.

Already emotionally spent, I yanked the door open and pulled the man out while telling Byron there was a gun between the front seats. I put the man down on the hood and handcuffed him while Byron did the same with the passenger, a mouthy eighteen-year-old punk. I retrieved the pistol and placed it in my truck. Knowing I didn't think it was a pistol I had heard fired, I returned to the vehicle. In the back seat between the fifteen-year-old girl and eleven-year-old boy was a camouflage sleeping bag. I told the boy to raise the sleeping bag, and as I suspected, it was concealing a .270 rifle. I carried the rifle and placed it in my truck. We wrote the two men tickets and allowed them to go on their way.

I shared with Byron how this was the most traumatic encounter I had ever had, thinking at first he had been shot and then thinking I was going to kill the driver in front of his kids. The realization the kids could have shot us while we had the violators on the hood was equally troubling. He admitted he had not been too excited until he saw me with my pistol screwed into the man's ear and yelling for him not to touch it. Although we went back to the decoy and monitored the area for a while longer, I had had enough excitement to last me for quite some time. As a matter of fact, even having a night hunter fire a shot while we were chasing him years later didn't shake me up like this episode did. But that's another story!

I have often heard the statistic that wildlife enforcement officers are several times more likely to be assaulted than other law enforcement officers. I have told folks many times when I leave home in the morning there is no guarantee I will return. I always follow that by reminding them that is true for everyone.

We all know there are no guarantees about tomorrow. The Bible says today is the day of salvation. While your odds may be better than mine, there is a statistic out that says one out of every one people dies. The Savior is waiting to enter your heart. Don't put it off.

Mistaken Identity
(Who Are You, Really?)

PEOPLE PROBABLY THINK checking folks fishing from the bank is a pretty mundane activity for a conservation enforcement officer (CEO) and most of the time it is. As you read that sentence I can't help but believe you are picturing an old guy sitting on a bucket with his line in the water waiting on his float to start bobbing. While that is often the case, the reality is you never know what you may encounter. We have had numerous officers assaulted while checking fishermen. You would be surprised the lengths people will go to when they have failed to purchase a fishing license that cost thirteen dollars.

During the month of March, CEO Jerry Fincher was checking fishermen on the Coosa River below Logan Martin Dam. The crappie were biting and that's all you have to say to draw a crowd during spring in Alabama. Where I am from that is pronounced "croppy." Who wants to eat a fish called crappie? They are good eating fish and many folks pursue them with a passion.

Jerry worked his way along the bank checking for license, undersize fish and over the limit violations. While checking the creel of one individual, the officer found three fish below the nine-inch minimum size limit. Our fisheries section monitors our population of fish every year. Some species have a size limit. Normally a size limit prohibits anglers from taking small (young)

Mistaken Identity

fish. This allows those fish to make it to a size where they can reproduce and keep the population stable. Like all limits, this size restriction is in place to benefit the resource and thereby the angler. Unfortunately, many fishermen view the size limit as unnecessary and therefore ignore it. That's why we check.

Since these "short" fish were still alive, Jerry decided he would allow the man to return the fish to the lake and would issue a written warning for the undersize fish violation.

The fish were released and Jerry asked the man for his fishing license and driver's license. The subject told him he didn't have his driver's license but did have a fishing license and handed it over. The license looked as though it had been waded up and thrown away after having been through the washing machine a time or two. Since the license was illegible, Jerry asked the man for his birthdate and noticed he had considerable trouble in coming up with that information. What about you, do you know your birthdate? Most folks do. So, when we come across someone who just can't seem to remember theirs, it raises a red flag.

Although it was extremely difficult to read, Jerry finally made out the license number and called it in to the Montgomery dispatcher. The dispatcher called back and informed the officer the subject had a felony warrant for rape. Jerry ordered the man to get on the ground and moved in to handcuff him. Several onlookers thought this would be a good time to come to the aid of their comrade, however Jerry forcefully instructed them to keep their distance while he applied the handcuffs.

It is interesting how a set of steel bracelets can change a situation and the demeanor of the wearer. The violator was now repeatedly telling the officer, "I need to confess, I need to confess." The detainee decided it was time to come clean and began telling the officer the license he had given him was actually borrowed from a friend and he was not the man with the felony warrant. As you may have guessed this was somewhat akin to the fellow who just had an officer pull some dope out of his pocket and the violator claims they aren't his pants. While that is never true, in this case the illegal fisherman provided his correct information and it was determined he was not who he had initially claimed to be. However, a review of his record showed he was a wanted individual with an outstanding warrant. Fortunately for him the warrant was for a misdemeanor offence.

The man was charged with fishing without a license, borrowing a license, possession of undersized fish and giving false information to a law enforcement officer. Jerry transported the man to the county jail and once there served him with the outstanding warrant. A warrant for—fishing without a license! Sometimes it just isn't your day! At least he didn't have to fork over thirteen dollars for a license!

As the officer was preparing to leave the jail the man looked at him and said, I really screwed up, didn't I? It was not a question, it was an acknowledgement.

What about you? Are you really who you claim to be? You know and God knows. I've arrested several folks for saying they were someone they weren't. Giving a false name to law enforcement was a pet peeve of my first district judge. It would normally earn the offender a trip to jail. I once heard the judge explain to a defendant how he had put a man in jail because someone else had used the man's name. It grieved the judge that the fellow erroneously was denied his freedom for something he did not do. Are you really who you say you are? The day is coming when everything will come to light. It is appointed to man once to die and then the judgment. The judgment will be just and the verdict will be final. No matter who we may claim to be, we are all sinners, but the gift of God is eternal life through Jesus Christ. Choose Him today and enjoy real freedom.

Corroborating Evidence

IT WAS A BIT UNUSUAL for someone to confess to another violation in an effort to get out of the violation at hand. However, I had come to understand a lot of things in law enforcement didn't make a whole lot of sense, and this was just another example of that.

In response to complaints, I was working in the north end of the county on a road known as the Macedonia loop. The loop is approximately three miles long and is bordered primarily by pastureland. We received numerous complaints of road hunting and some night hunting there over the years.

While driving around the loop, I met my friend, Sheriff's Deputy Brett Oakes. We pulled over into a wide driveway and talked for a few minutes. As we shot the breeze, a vehicle approached from the east. The driver steered from one lane to the other allowing their headlights to illuminate the fields on each side of the road. I told Brett, "They are shining with their headlights." Oddly enough they passed our location, where we were sitting within twenty yards of the road, and continued to shine in the same manner.

Many folks are under the erroneous assumption that anyone night hunting uses a spotlight to spot their target. While this is very often true, in our heavily forested county we experienced a tremendous amount of "ditch shooting," where folks spotted deer just off the roadway using only the headlights on their vehicle. In addition, as in this case, when there were some fields or pastures available, they could be viewed by the driver manipulating their vehicle so their headlights would light up the area. This was an effective technique that lessened the chance of apprehension. While seeing a vehicle turned crossways in the road would obviously tip us off to what was going on, you had to be able to see the vehicle. On the other hand, we could spot someone using a spotlight from miles away.

I pulled out and began to follow the slow-moving truck down the road. We were moving at a very slow pace, and the driver continued to maneuver the vehicle so the headlights were shining the fields along the roadside. After following them for a few minutes, I decided the driver might not be hunting but was in all likelihood drunk. After all, I was following him with my headlights on, and I would think this would have altered the behavior of anyone who was attempting to "shine" deer and was aware someone was behind them. I called the deputy and asked him to come to my location. Within a minute, Brett was behind me. I activated my blue lights, which received no reaction whatsoever. This lack of response reinforced my notion the driver was probably intoxicated. As we approached a crossroads with a stop sign, I activated my siren. The driver immediately slammed on the brakes and I realized he had obviously been unaware I had been behind him for a mile. I was pretty sure he was drunk, and I told Brett if he would take the driver, I would get the passenger.

Although my first inclination had been these folks were night hunting, I had now dismissed that idea. Therefore, you can imagine the look on my face when I opened the passenger's door and there between him and the door was a shotgun that turned out to be loaded with buckshot! After determining there were no more weapons in the vehicle, I carried the shotgun back and placed it in my truck.

I advised the passenger of his rights and questioned him. When I asked why he had the shotgun, his first response was he didn't know it was in the truck. Although I know it was unprofessional, I literally laughed out loud. I told him there was no way whatsoever he could have gotten in or out of the truck without moving the gun. Realizing the truth of my statement, he simply hung his head. I again asked why he had the gun, and he replied his brother-in-law, the driver, had asked him to bring it.

"Why would he ask you to do that?" I asked, and he replied he guessed it was in case they saw a deer to shoot. I informed him riding around with a loaded shotgun looking for deer to shoot constituted night hunting, and he nodded his head. I requested he give me a written statement. He roughed out a statement and signed it.

I went to where Brett was talking with the driver and was surprised to learn he was not intoxicated. I advised him of his rights and told him that based on his shining the fields with his headlights and possessing a loaded shotgun, it was my contention he was hunting at night. He quickly declared, "I don't night hunt." I again stated I felt he was night hunting, and he again denied it. As I allowed his statement to hang in the air, I saw a light suddenly come on in his eyes, and he proceeded to tell me he didn't need to night hunt. He proudly claimed he had killed four does that morning, and he added there was nothing I could do about it because it was doe days.

Years ago, before the either-sex season became an everyday-of-the-season thing, counties would have a few days when does could be killed. The limit during this time was one doe per day. Although it was doe season in Coosa County, this guy had obviously exceeded the bag limit. Of course, in those days I was eager to write a ticket, and the wheels in my head started turning. Acting as if I was confused, I told him I needed to get this straight. I said,

"You are saying you don't need to be out here night hunting because you killed four does this morning?"

"That's right," was his quick reply.

I asked, "Would you sign a statement to that effect?"

He said, "Yes."

I prepared the statement and he signed it. I prepared a bond for night hunting and told him he was under arrest for night hunting. Although he still claimed to be innocent, he signed his bond and was on his way.

I knew since I had not witnessed the over-the-limit violation I would have to obtain a warrant in order to arrest him; however, I was about to learn a valuable lesson concerning the law. I was feeling pretty proud of myself for being able to obtain a confession for a blatant violation I had no knowledge of previously.

You've heard the phrase "proud as a peacock"; well, my feathers were about to be clipped. I approached the assistant district attorney (ADA) to secure a warrant. I told him I had arrested the man for night hunting and also wanted to obtain a warrant for exceeding the bag limit on deer for the four does he admitted killing earlier in the day. The ADA looked at me and asked, "Did you see the deer?" I replied I had not seen the deer, but I had advised the defendant of his rights prior to him giving me a statement admitting killing them.

The ADA asked how I knew he had really killed the deer. I replied, "Because he said he did."

He asked, "Did he say he was night hunting?"

I said, "No, he denied it."

"But you arrested him anyway?"

"Yes, but I saw that."

The ADA said, "He told you he wasn't night hunting, and you didn't believe him, and he told you he killed four does, and you did believe him?"

Corroborating Evidence

I was becoming more than a little uneasy with our conversation, and I attempted to bring it back to the matter at hand. "He confessed to killing the does after being advised of his rights," I again stated. I learned a lesson that served me well for the remainder of my career. Evidently, in almost every case, you must have a corpus delicti, "the body of the crime." Without the body of the crime, it is difficult to prove there was a crime.

I had learned early on people can and will say and do anything. Rarely did I believe much of what a defendant had to say since I was so accustomed to being lied to. This propensity of violators to have an aversion against telling the truth was the reason I needed corroborating evidence. I did not obtain the warrant.

I proceeded to court with only the night hunting charges. The cases were called, and the defendants and I approached the bench. The defendants pled not guilty, so the judge had us raise our hands to be sworn in. He asked me what had occurred, and I told him the story. I also gave him the signed statement the passenger had given. As was his custom, the judge asked the defendants if they would like to ask me any questions or make any statements. The passenger stepped up to the bench and said, "Judge, I never should have signed that paper."

I'm not sure, but I think the judge, like me, was trying not to laugh when he said, "Well it's a little late to say that now." He found both defendants guilty.

The driver said, "But I don't night hunt," and the judge replied, "You were that night. You're in the custody of the sheriff." The man was still claiming his innocence as the deputy took him by the arm and led him to the holding box.

That was my first encounter with corroborating evidence, but it would not be the last. I made better cases after that day.

I can easily relate this case to someone claiming to be a Christian. The Bible is clear that I am not to judge whether or not someone else is a Christian. However, it is also clear when it says everyone should be able to spot a Christian based on their actions. What about you? Is there any corroborating evidence in your life that would lead a reasonable and prudent person to believe you are a follower of Christ? There needs to be!

Best Friends

"Do you know [insert warden's name]? He's my best friend." I have no way of knowing, but I believe it's a good bet that every officer has had someone say that to them. This normally occurs when the person being encountered by the officer believes they are likely to be in trouble. While that is the norm, there are always exceptions to every rule.

Responding to a hunting without a permit complaint, CEO Sgt. Keith Mann encountered a couple of outlaws who, while new to him, were well known by me and my cohort Gene Carver, as we had arrested them previously. That made it all the better when Keith called Gene and told him the guys had informed him that he was their best friend and would have been hunting with them if he didn't have to work!

Living close to Montgomery, our state capital, as I did for my entire career had a few drawbacks. Since it was the location of our state office, we were often a little too handy for various details that arose. In addition, Montgomery was the site of many events we were required to work. One of the largest events was the Buckmasters Expo, which would normally have as many as thirty thousand people pass through.

While working our booth, I had a fellow tell me the warden in his county was his best friend. Expecting that I would know the officer, I asked, "Who is it?" The man spent the next five minutes trying to come up with his best friend's name! He eventually walked away still unable to come up with it.

CEO Earl Brown (retired) was wearing a vest that concealed his name tag one cool fall afternoon while checking bank fishing on the rocks below Mitchell Dam. He checked a fellow's license and found everything to be in order. As he prepared to move to the next person, the guy asked him if he knew Earl Brown. He replied that he did, and the man said, "Earl Brown tried to check my license one day, and I whipped him."

Of course, this flew all over Earl, and he immediately got right in the man's face and said, "Well here he stands, why don't you do it again?" The man was mumbling something about it must have been someone else as he quickly gathered his gear and headed toward his vehicle.

While working night hunting CEO Jerry Fincher was monitoring the SO radio and heard a call concerning a man armed with a screwdriver holding someone hostage at a local boat landing. The deputies were unsure of the location of the landing, so Jerry advised he would meet them and lead them in. When the vehicles pulled up, the obviously drunken assailant took off running and jumped into a car and locked the doors. The officers surrounded the vehicle and ordered the man out. He opened the door, surrendered his screwdriver, and drunkenly tried to explain the situation. Spotting Jerry standing in the crowd, he asked him if he knew Jerry Fincher. Jerry replied he did know him. The man then proclaimed that Jerry Fincher and his wife were his two best friends in the world!

With the deputies looking at Jerry in disbelief he advised them he had never seen the man before. With the situation under control and no one wanting to press any charges, the deputies decided to allow one of the man's real friends to drive him home.

Best Friends

As they were pulling away, the driver stopped the vehicle and got out. When the deputy asked what he was doing, he replied he was getting his buddy another beer. You can't make this stuff up!

Working thirty plus years as a wildlife biologist and CEO, I was fortunate to make many friends. I'm sure if I could talk to all of the officers in the state, I'd probably learn of some other friends, ones I've never even heard of.

Let me tell you that for a law enforcement officer, someone asking "Don't I know you?" carries a different connotation than for other folks. When someone asks that, we start searching through our memory bank trying to remember is this a landowner I've helped along the way or someone I helped send to prison, and do I need to start reaching for my handgun? This is a common occurrence. In my career, I have encountered thousands of folks, and I will tell you my hard drive is nearly full and my retrieval system has started to develop some glitches.

Probably like many of you when talking about a memorable event, I have used the expression "I'll never forget it." I surely don't plan to forget; however, there may come a day when that is out of my control. I want to tell you a sad story with a happy ending.

In January of 2016, my wife and I traveled to Tucson, Arizona, to attend the National Wild Turkey Symposium. It was a great trip up until I got the call that my dad had been taken to the hospital by ambulance and was not doing well. We flew home and made the two-hundred-mile drive to the hospital. I found my dad confused and agitated. His words were slurred, and he was totally frustrated. When I spoke with the physicians, their tone was accusatory. Their questions centered around why my dad was living on his own with my elderly mother in their rural home without professional nursing assistance. I explained how only days earlier my dad was in good condition, caring for himself and my mother, attending to chores around the house, and fully coherent. They acted as if they did not believe that; however, I knew it was the truth. I asked what their test had revealed, and they stated he was dehydrated. While I knew dehydration was bad, I felt there was more to his condition.

Days later, it was decided Daddy would need to go to a nursing home for a twenty-one-day stay to recover. At the nursing home, I met with their physician, whose first question was, "When did your dad have his stroke?" I replied no one had told me he had had a stroke. The doctor looked at me and said, "Oh yes, he has definitely had a stroke."

Although Daddy did regain many of his abilities, the lingering effect of the stroke, coupled with his Parkinson's disease, dictated that he would need to remain in the nursing home. Some days were worse than others, but he normally was fairly sharp. However, over time, I would sometimes wonder whether or not he really recognized me. I would simply ask, "Who am I?" and he would act a little disgusted and say, "Joel." At other times, I would point to my wife and ask, "Who is this?" and he would immediately respond, "Melanie."

Unfortunately, a few months later, Dad suffered another light stroke. Recognition was still there but becoming more difficult. Then came the day when Daddy was really failing, and I asked him if he knew me, and he looked at me with those sweet but now scared eyes, and he said, "No." I died a little that day as my heart was broken and my spirit crushed.

Not long after that, I was on patrol with the Coosa County SO when I received a call from the nursing home saying Dad had taken a turn for the worse, and I needed to get up there. I called and told my wife to get ready, and we made the two-hundred-mile trip, arriving at 4:00 a.m. It was very hard to tell whether or not Daddy ever recognized me. A few days later, as I held his frail hand, he peacefully slipped into the arms of Jesus.

I'm sure that many reading these words can relate to this story. Losing a parent cuts deep and stays with you. It's sad but not the saddest thing that can happen. I experienced peace knowing that my dad knew the Lord as his Savior. I take comfort in knowing I will see my dad again, and there will be no more tears. Whether or not my dad knew me was really insignificant. What was important was he knew Jesus and Jesus knew him. To me, one of the most hard-hitting verses in the Bible is found at Matthew 7:21–23. "Not everyone who says to Me, 'Lord, Lord,' shall enter the kingdom of heaven, but he who does the will of My Father in heaven. Many will say to Me in that day, 'Lord, Lord, have we not prophesied in Your name, cast out demons in Your name, and done many wonders in Your name?' And then I will declare to them, 'I never knew you; depart from Me, you who practice lawlessness!'"

In these verses the people (church people) are pleading with Jesus on the Day of Judgment, saying we were in church every week, we did this and that, and so on, and Jesus says, "Depart from me, for I never knew you."

The story of my dad dying is a sad one, but it doesn't hold a candle to realizing you will be spending eternity in hell separated from Jesus. You definitely have the opportunity to change your fate, now. The Savior is waiting to enter your heart. Accept His offer today.

Just like the officers I discussed in this story, you may or may not know who your friends are, but I know who it needs to be. What a friend we have in Jesus.

Disposition

EARLY IN MY CAREER, hunting deer with the aid of dogs was very popular in Coosa County. There were numerous dog hunting clubs and other loosely organized groups that hunted the open permit land that was readily available. Although I worked a management area hunt almost every weekend of the deer season, the two conservation enforcement officers (CEO) and myself spent many Saturdays and Sundays going from one dog hunting complaint to the next. The calls ranged from the landowner who heard dogs running on his property to the driver who had passed numerous armed men standing in the roadway. Dog hunters also registered complaints with the most common one being their belief someone had shot one of their dogs. Dog hunters loved their deer dogs and when someone even thought their dog had been shot, emotions ran high.

I could understand how a landowner who had spent thousands of dollars obtaining property and thousands more improving the habitat for wildlife would be upset when their tranquil hunt was rudely interrupted by a pack of dogs. While there were rogue dog hunters who intentionally ran dogs across neighboring properties, the main problem seemed to occur when folks tried to run dogs on a small acreage. Obviously, dogs don't recognize property lines and can't read no trespassing signs. Therefore, conflicts were bound to happen.

Disposition

With the complaints about the dogs remaining steady and sometimes increasing, the public demanded something be done. Therefore, Coosa and Chambers Counties became the first counties to be placed on the dog hunting permit system. To acquire a permit, hunting clubs had to provide the conservation department with maps of their property and a membership roster. The clubs were issued a number and each dog had to have the number on its collar. Theoretically when someone caught dogs running on their property we could identify which club was the culprit. We kept records of complaints and clubs with numerous complaints could be placed on probation or have their permit revoked. Although not perfect, the system did help alleviate some of the problems.

Prior to each season, clubs would have to submit updated maps, membership rosters and a form that asked if any members had been arrested for game law violations during the previous year and, if so, the disposition of the cases. The CEOs and I would review these documents prior to the hunting season and make recommendations concerning the club's status.

One year while looking over the application of the county's largest hunting club I noticed they had a couple of members who had been arrested the previous year. Not being familiar with the cases, I was interested in what they had been charged with and the disposition. While just about everyone understood what it meant to be arrested, evidently the definition of disposition was a little more elusive. The report stated the two men had received tickets for hunting without a permit. Hunting without permission of the landowner was a fairly prevalent charge in Alabama where all land is posted by law. Landowners are not required to post any signs or even have their boundaries marked. It is the responsibility of the hunter to know where they are at all times.

Any person who hunts, traps, captures, injures, kills, or destroys, or attempts to hunt, trap, capture, injure, kill, or destroy any wild game on the lands of another between the hours of daylight and sunset without the written permission of or accompanied by the landowner or person in possession or control of the lands shall be guilty of a misdemeanor and, upon conviction, shall be punished for the first offense by a fine of not less than one thousand dollars ($1,000), and at the discretion of the court may have all hunting license privileges revoked for up to one year from the date of conviction. Any person shall be punished for the second and each subsequent offense by a fine of not less than two thousand dollars ($2,000) and the revocation of all hunting license privileges for one year from the date of conviction, and shall be imprisoned in the county jail for a period not less than ten nor more than thirty days.

As you can see we take hunting without permission seriously and rightfully so. While it is a serious violation it would not necessarily cause the revocation of the club's permit. Of course, it depended on the disposition of the case. If the fellows were found not guilty it would be a moot point. When I found the disposition section of the form it turned out to be very interesting but not at all what I had anticipated. While I expected to see guilty or not guilty, that wasn't what I found. On the disposition line it read, friendly and easy to get along with! You can't make this stuff up.

What about you, do you understand what your disposition is? Where do you stand? Have you accepted the free pardon of sin Jesus offers? Do you go to church with your wife occasionally? Maybe you make it on Easter or Mother's Day or Christmas. Jesus isn't interested in a half-hearted commitment. He says it's all or nothing. He is looking for a committed relationship with Him. Many folks play church every week yet do not know the Savior. If the guys in the hunting club were to describe your disposition would it include the word Christian? Think about it.

Compassion

WHILE IN GRADUATE SCHOOL at Mississippi State University (MSU), I normally always enjoyed when we would have a guest lecturer. The folks were usually good speakers, and it was interesting hearing what we had to look forward to in the "real" world. That may be the reason I enjoyed going back and speaking to classes for twenty-four years! I appreciate my dear friends Drs. Jeanne and Daryl Jones affording me those opportunities.

One day our guest lecturer was Dave Holloway. Mr. Holloway was an MSU grad who had gone on to a successful career with the US Fish and Wildlife Service as a special agent, which is a federal game warden. Some of you may recall several years ago, before game warden shows were common, there was a documentary on television entitled *Wildlife Wars* that exposed the illegal wildlife exploits of outlaws from across the country. A lot of the footage shown had been shot by Special Agent Holloway. He explained to our class his method of covert law enforcement was to overtly pose as an outdoor writer with a video camera. He told how more often than not the outlaws would receive him with open arms and enjoyed him filming their illegal exploits. Of course, he also did some deep undercover work in some very volatile and dangerous situations. He relayed how he had sat at a table and negotiated with the leader of an outlaw biker gang. On the table was the skull of the man's girlfriend, whom he had killed because he thought she had reported some of his illegal activities to the authorities. The skull was a not-so-subtle reminder to others what happened to a snitch.

At this time, I knew very little about wildlife law enforcement. I had been checked by a game warden once in my life. I admit I was astounded listening to the hair-raising near-death experiences dealing with the lowest of the low and laying his life on the line on a daily basis. He had worked everywhere from the levees in Louisiana to ice floes in Alaska. His stories were great. As his lecture drew to a conclusion, he used the line I had heard several times. He said, "If you don't remember anything else, remember this."

Seeing how this lecturer was different than any I had ever heard, I knew the "take-home" message would be a good one. I was not disappointed; however, I was somewhat confused. After having listened to how he spent day after day dealing with wildlife violators and those who would just as soon shoot you as not, I fully anticipated his advice would be either always carry a backup gun or always wear your bulletproof vest or grow a second set of eyes in the back of your head like your second-grade teacher had. However, none of those was correct. His take-home message was about as far to the other end of the spectrum as I could imagine. He said, "When dealing with these people, always have compassion." Talk about a surprise ending! I surely never saw that one coming. I had been so into his talk, yet I left the room scratching my head.

Fast forward a few years, and I found myself being threatened, called every name in the book, and even shot at. It soon became evident I was going to have to give up umpiring Little League baseball! Truthfully, I did umpire Little League baseball for fifteen years, and it did get pretty rough at times. I digress. Actually,

Compassion

about one year after the lecture, I was in fact on the front line of wildlife law enforcement. Working overtly, I was astonished on a daily basis. I could not believe the lengths people would go to breaking the laws and regulations. I was dealing with a bunch of outlaws on a regular basis, and having compassion for them wasn't even on my radar. How on earth do you have compassion for folks who lie to your face, slander you behind your back, and threaten to shoot you? No, compassion was not even in the equation.

Through my early career, I would recall Mr. Holloway's words, and I would try my best to figure out just what he meant. How do you have compassion for people who leave home every day bent on breaking the law? Who lie about you and bring false accusations against you? They taunt you with their lawlessness. They accuse you of having no compassion because you are arresting them when you could have let them go. How do you have compassion on these people? Thankfully, not everyone we dealt with fell into this outlaw category, but believe me when I tell you it was prevalent. While there were a lot of good, law-abiding hunters, they weren't the ones we had to spend most of our time on.

One day it finally dawned on me. I began to realize I often treated these people differently than some other officers. Although many were hardened outlaws who might shoot their own mother much less me, I treated them with as much respect as they would allow. After my two training officers retired and I began to take on that role, I often found myself telling the new officers to treat people as nicely as they would allow you to. Granted, sometimes they would not let you treat them very nicely. However, many of the violators were basically good people who had made a mistake. They weren't out either to kill me or to do irreparable damage to the resource. However, they did need to be apprehended and face the consequences of their wrongdoing.

As crazy as it sounded to me when Mr. Holloway said it, I began to understand I needed to do my best to show Jesus to these folks. I did not say it was easy, nor did I always succeed, but I did begin to understand about compassion.

Something I also taught all the officers I had an opportunity to "train" was that if, when you finish writing a violator tickets that will likely cost him $3,000 to $4,000 and you seize his gun, he shakes your hand and says, "Thank you," you have done a good job. I had that happen many times. They were not saying they appreciated the tickets; they were saying they appreciated the way they were treated.

I believe people are called into many professions. These would include the clergy, teaching, hospice care, and law enforcement. Remember there are people in these professions that are not called to them. They are the ones who give the occupations a bad name.

The Bible tells me God is a God of order not chaos. Law enforcement officers are in place to keep the peace. In this dangerous world, these officers often enforce the peace by apprehending the law breakers. How is arresting and/or jailing people showing compassion for them? The book of Romans says the authorities are God's servants. They are there to protect you; however, if you are doing wrong, you should be afraid, for they have the power to punish you. God has called us to obey all duly appointed authority.

Today our news is rampant with reports of officers abusing their authority and making bad choices. Some of the accusations are true, and many are not. Many claim officers are not held accountable for their actions. Again, this isn't normally true; however, there is a truth everyone should remember. The Bible says we should obey and submit to authorities, for they are keeping watch over you, and they will give an account for it.

COMPASSION

People resent authority, including law enforcement, and especially those who enforce laws and regulations governing people's recreation like wildlife officers do. Hebrews 12:11 says, "No chastening for the moment seems enjoyable, but painful. But afterwards, to those who have been trained by it, it yields the peaceful fruit of righteousness."

So how do you reconcile being compassionate and enforcing the law? Well, it isn't easy, but it helps knowing God ordains law enforcement. Midway through my career as a law enforcement officer, I finally realized I treated people with compassion as much for me as for them. Is there someone you need to show some compassion to?

As weird as it may sound, I learned a lot from a game warden I never met. His name was Lt. Alton Boulware. He was the first partner of one of my first partners, Hershel Patterson. Hershel would often offer some sage advice by saying, "Alton always told me…" One bit of that advice was if you don't feel right about writing somebody a ticket, don't do it. That had something to do with compassion and something to do with being able to live with yourself. Both of those things were and are important.

By the Grace of God

It continued to amaze me how Coosa County seemed to be a magnet for night hunters. This was surprising to me in that our district judge was well known for hammering violators, handing out hefty fines and confiscating firearms. It wasn't unusual for the judge to assess fines and court costs totaling tens of thousands of dollars each month during deer season. However, unlike today when deer are common throughout the state, at this time Coosa had a much higher deer population than did surrounding counties. Therefore, when folks were headed to the southern part of the state to deer hunt, ours was the first place they would start seeing deer standing alongside the road. And a deer standing beside the road just proved too much of a temptation for many.

With night hunting so prevalent, at least once or twice each season we would request assistance from officers in the surrounding counties in an attempt to saturate the county and hopefully apprehend a few of the culprits. One of these nights is etched in my memory. It was a night I'll never forget, and I'm thankful I survived.

Our departmental covert officer and I had already had a good night catching two night hunters and taking them to the county jail after a high-speed chase. We had finally finished all of the paperwork associated with that type situation and decided to give the other side of the county a try. It was 1:00 a.m. when we headed to Alabama Highway 259 near the Fishpond community to try our luck. Although our departmental policy stated we would not use the decoy on a main highway, our supervisor had determined that after midnight very few highways were main highways in rural Alabama. Highway 259 was a perennial night hunting favorite. As a matter of fact, we were going to set up in the very spot where I had caught the first night hunters of my career when I had been working only six days! I had not yet been issued a gun and had received no training whatsoever. Looking back, I realize I only survived by the grace of God. This reality was about to once again be brought to my attention in a very real way.

We soon arrived and set up the decoy deer and settled into our hiding spot. A good hiding/observation location was a cherished thing when working the decoy. We had located a real gem along this highway. We could back in between two earthen banks and had a great view of a wide roadside. It was a quintessential night hunting setup.

This was early in my career, and we were using one of the prototype decoys. This decoy was not, however, the original stationary buck; this was an advanced prototype with a moveable tail and a device that enabled us to cause the deer to fall after someone shot it. As with most innovations, necessity was the mother of invention. We had learned early on that after someone shot the stationary deer and it didn't even flinch, it wasn't long until you were in a high-speed chase (as a matter of fact it had occurred earlier that night). The knockdown device caused the shooter to believe the deer was down, and most would pull to the side of the road, giving us an opportunity to make the apprehension. The knockdown device was what my major professor in graduate school would have called a Rube Goldberg contraption. It consisted of a piece of plywood, a steel trap, a piece of inner tube, a metal spike, and a remote control trigger. Rube Goldberg or not, it worked very well!

At about 2:30 a.m. a slow-moving, small pickup eased its way down the highway. The driver slowed to a stop with his headlights shining on the fake deer. We waited with bated breath. However, instead of hearing a shot, I heard the driver whistle. This was a first for me. I had had people blow their horn at, yell at, take pictures of, and even try to hit the decoy with a bumper jack (I'm not making this up), but I had never had someone simply whistle at it. The decoy had been in use for a few years, and this was this poacher's way of being sure he wasn't fooled. "He's whistling at it," I told my partner. "He's not going to shoot it." He held his finger to his lips telling me to keep quiet. The driver again whistled at the deer. My cohort activated the remote control lever and made the decoy's tail wiggle from side to side. BOOM!! Instantly a shot rang out. Manipulating the other switch caused the deer to hit the ground.

Although this normally stopped the shooter, this guy eased off and drove down the road. This was a night for firsts. I had never had a night hunter to shoot and then casually drive away. I had seen several stop the vehicle and start getting out, and when using the deer that didn't fall, I had seen several tear out like their hair was on fire! This guy casually drove off.

We were soon right behind the guy with our blue lights flashing. To my further astonishment he continued to drive down the road like we weren't even there! We were only moving at about thirty-five miles per hour, and the suspect obviously wasn't attempting to elude; however, he wasn't stopping. After about a minute, which seemed like an hour, the suspect pulled to the right side of the road. We exited our truck and approached the vehicle. As fate would have it and due to my youthful exuberance, I approached ahead of my partner and on the passenger side of the vehicle. As I eased up to the door, I noticed the driver's head was turned and he was looking out the open driver-side window. I looked in the passenger-side window and observed something I can still vividly see today. The subject was holding onto the steering wheel with his left hand. In the bend of his arm lay his Remington pump action 30-06 rifle with the barrel pointing out the window. The suspect's right hand was holding the stock of the gun, and his finger was on the trigger! I immediately turned and motioned for my partner to stay back. The guy had never seen me or anticipated anyone coming up on the passenger side of the truck. Realizing he would not be able to swing the gun around inside the cab of the truck, I opened the passenger-side door and snatched the rifle away from the startled man. I also grabbed the fully loaded 12-gauge shotgun that was lying in the passenger seat.

My partner approached and took the man out of the truck. We arrested him for hunting at night and from a public road. He signed his bonds and was allowed to go on his way.

Later we would learn he had previously been arrested for several wildlife law violations, including killing two illegal deer, for which he served six months in jail. I think his plan was not to go back!

Never had I knowingly been so close to someone being shot. There is no doubt in my mind the subject had every intention of shooting the officer as he walked up to the window. I've often thought had things been different, if I had been working by myself as I often did, or if I had approached on the driver's side as I normally did, my career may well have ended lying in Highway 259 at 2:35 a.m.

The subject was found guilty in district court. And was later caught again, hunting without a permit in an adjacent county.

About a year after this incident occurred, someone placed a mobile home in the area, which kept us from being able to use the decoy there. A while later the county took down one of the earthen banks we hid behind, rendering the site useless for us. However, I passed through the area many times during the remainder of my career, and each time I remembered how close we had come to dying that night.

As I mentioned earlier, I pen these words only by the grace of a living God. If you don't know Him, you shouldn't let this day end without changing that situation. You may be like I was and may be closer to the end of your life than you realize! Just like our primo night hunting spot that soon disappeared, Jesus said his spirit will not always strive with man. Today is the day of salvation. Make your decision before it's too late. Jesus saves. I praise his holy name!

My partner that night went on to be the first head of the departmental covert unit. He worked many high-dollar, high-stress cases all over the country. He was in more tense situations than anyone should ever be in. He spent his career laying it on the line for wildlife. He made it through it all without a scratch, and so did I. By the grace of God.

Does It Make Any Difference?

WHEN I BEGAN MY LAW ENFORCEMENT CAREER, I was introduced to the two county game wardens. One of them told me I would learn more in six months of working with them than I did in my entire college career. Seeing how I had just finished six years of college, I was a little skeptical about that; however, after six months, I found he was correct in many ways.

One of the first things the officers relayed to me was if I saw a vehicle with a thirty-one or fifty county tag, I could get ready to write a ticket. I must admit this type of stereotyping made me a little uncomfortable. I think that was true in part because the officers tended to group everyone from "north Alabama" in the same category. That bothered me, seeing how I was from as far north Alabama as you could get. However, after working for just a few weeks, I began to realize what they meant about the thirty-one and fifty county tags. It seemed every time we stopped someone from Etowah or Marshall County, we did end up writing a ticket.

In addition to grouping all north Alabamians together, the officers also educated me concerning certain individuals as well. One of these individuals was known as "the preacher." They told me the preacher was part of the original bunch from "north Alabama" and to watch him close and not believe anything he said. I once again had some trouble with this. I grew up in church all my life, and, while I know preachers are just people, I do my best to respect them until I find a reason not to.

As fate would have it, the opening day of the spring turkey season found me working alone on the Coosa WMA. By this time, I was a fairly seasoned officer with almost two months under my belt! I was checking hunters on the ridge road and soon stopped a Ford pickup. I asked the driver for his license and permit and told him I would like to examine his firearm. As I checked the gun to make sure it was unloaded, he retrieved his licenses and gave them to me. As I viewed the license, I noted they were current, and I also noted the name on the license: it was the preacher from north Alabama. I asked to see his management area permit, and he searched his wallet for it. Not finding it, he began to search a little more frantically through the truck.

After a few minutes, I asked to see his driver's license and began writing him a ticket. As I wrote the ticket, he explained how he wished I would give him a break because he had worked for years to clean up the name of people from north Alabama, and this would tear down all of his work. As I finished writing the ticket and gave it to him to sign, he made one last attempt to get out of the citation. He said, "I know it doesn't make any difference, but worst of all, I'm a Baptist preacher."

To that, I responded, "You're right."

This response sort of surprised him, and he asked, "What do you mean I'm right?"

I said, "You are right when you said it doesn't make any difference."

With that, he signed the ticket and went on his way.

Later that day I noticed his vehicle once again approaching my position. I eyed him cautiously as he pulled up and presented me with a management area permit. He said he had gone to the store and obtained it and wanted me to know he had it. I told him that was fine, but it did not undo the fact he did not have it when I had checked him earlier.

When I told the man it didn't make any difference that he was a preacher, I was indicating that the law should apply equally to everyone. I was not implying that whether or not someone is a Christian doesn't make a difference. Have I ever arrested any Christians? Yes. Christians aren't perfect, but true Christians are forgiven. What difference does it make that you are a Christian?

Being deceived by others is serious, but deceiving yourself is even worse. Those who hear the word of God and do not follow its teachings are deceiving themselves into thinking they are Christians when they are not.

The book of James says people should be able to identify a Christian by their good works. He said your lifestyle should let people know whether or not you are a child of God. That is not to say you will never make a mistake. Some people in James's day thought observing holy days and feasts, attending worship services, and praying and fasting were signs of true spirituality. James, however, said a better evidence of a truly religious person is controlling his tongue.

Merely listening to spiritual truth or engaging in formal religious activity is not enough. The person who has real faith practices spiritual truth, loves others, and lives a holy life before God. Jesus said, "Not everyone that says to me Lord, Lord, shall enter unto the kingdom of heaven, but he that doeth the will of my Father, who is in heaven... And I will profess to them depart from me for I never knew you." Does it make a difference that you are a Christian? Your eternal life depends on it.

The preacher appeared in court the following month. When his case was called, we both approached the judge's bench. The judge asked how he would plead, and he responded, "Not guilty." I was sworn in by the judge and testified as to what had happened. The preacher testified that what I had said was true, but he had obtained a permit as soon as he could and hoped the judge would take that into consideration.

The judge barely hesitated in finding the preacher not guilty. I know I did a poor job of hiding my disbelief. I was shocked that a defendant could come into court and admit he was guilty yet be found not guilty. Although he did not have to justify his ruling, the judge offered a brief explanation, saying the defendant had in effect rectified the situation by obtaining the necessary permit, although after the fact, and no one was hurt in the situation. I must admit I may not have been hurt by it; however, it did leave a very bitter taste in my mouth. I can literally count on both hands the number of cases I ever lost in court.

Does it make a difference that you are a Christian? We need to examine what happened during the adjudication of this case. The defendant was charged, came to judgment, admitted his guilt, yet walked away free. That puts in mind of some verses in Romans that say all have sinned and come short of the glory of God. And then another that says the wages of sin is death, but the gift of God is eternal life through Jesus Christ, our Lord. That's a powerful verse; however, I think many people miss an extremely important part of it. It's easy to dwell on the gift of eternal life, and that is a great promise; however, it is important to realize who that promise is to. The verse ends saying through Jesus Christ, OUR Lord. Therefore, I feel that verse implies that if Jesus Christ isn't your Lord, then eternal life (in heaven) isn't yours. Does it make a difference that you are a Christian? If asked that question, I think people must ask themselves, "Does my life positively demonstrate I'm a Christian? Is there any evidence?"

Again?

HAVE YOU EVER HAD A MOMENT when you had to look around and see if anyone had observed what had just happened? You tripped and almost fell while going across a parking lot or maybe knocked several items off the shelf at the grocery store. Maybe you had just stunk up an elevator when the door opened and your boss stepped on. Maybe you walked past a wildlife law violator who possessed a lethal weapon and who knew if you spotted them you would either take them into custody or issue them citations that would cost them hundreds or thousands of dollars. I think that probably trumps the other examples. I have experienced that a few times.

The illegal baiting of wildlife was nearly epidemic during my entire career. As a matter of fact, there were several attempts to legalize the activity and eventually it was legalized to an extent. Deer, turkey, and dove were routinely baited in my area of east central Alabama and across the entire state. I always enjoyed catching someone hunting over bait, especially turkey bait. To me, those who would lure in and shoot a wild turkey over bait were the lowest of the low. I guess I took it very personally seeing how I enjoyed turkey hunting so much. Of course, I enjoyed catching deer hunters over bait as well. However, it was not lost on me that working bait was one of the most dangerous things we did.

Many times we received information telling us an area was baited. At other times we simply went on a gut feeling. The gut feeling was often developed by our observation of a lot of activity on a certain road or in a particular area. My partner, Hershel Patterson, and I had received information some guys were not only hunting over bait, but were doing so in a safety zone on Coosa WMA where no hunting was allowed. The suspected culprits actually owned the property that bordered the safety zone. This meant we would have to access the area from the WMA side, which meant a pretty long walk. We made our way into the safety zone toward the suspect's property line and soon located a couple of feed blocks buried in the ground.

I must tell you I have seen a little bit of everything used to bait wildlife. This includes, but is definitely not limited to, peanut butter, cottonseed hulls, peas, sweet potatoes, corn, wheat, and birdseed. Midway through my career there was a court ruling that changed the way we worked bait. Previously our law and regulation stated an area was considered to be baited for ten days after all feed had been removed. We need not prove the folks hunting the area knew the bait was present. However, a court ruling changed that to say the violator knew or should have known the area was baited. This meant we either had to have some evidence the person hunting had actually placed the bait there or the bait had to be visible to a person hunting who would make a reasonable overview of the area. If you were sitting there in plain view of a feeder or corn on the ground you were in violation. If the corn had been gone for a couple of days then you might not be in violation. Things were no longer nearly as simple for us.

In this case, the fellows we were after had purchased something relatively new at the time, a feed block consisting of corn and molasses and supposedly other minerals fashioned into a square block. We always liked to find these blocks because it normally meant the area would be baited until we caught the people since the block did not weather much and evidently it took the wildlife a long time to consume it.

Further investigation of the area around the blocks revealed two trees that had obviously been climbed several times with climbing tree stands. We also located what appeared to be a well-used trail that led to the private property bordering the WMA. We decided this would be a good time to check out the private property. It was on the private property that we hit the mother lode of bait. We found hanging and trough feeders filled with corn with permanent tree stands overlooking each site. We took samples of the bait and hurriedly left the area and waited for the weekend.

Saturday morning found us once again walking into the safety zone looking for the illegal hunters. As I cautiously entered the baited area, I slowly scanned each tree looking for the bow hunter. Easing through the area, I began to get one of those feelings that I'm sure most officers have had at one time or another. The one where the hair on the back of your neck stands up and you feel the eyeballs on you. Having felt that way before, I immediately stopped and once again scanned the trees. This closer look revealed I had walked directly under the camo-clad bow hunter! It took a few seconds for me to regain my composure realizing he could have easily sent an arrow right through me. I instructed him to lower his bow and safely come down the tree. Once he was on the ground, I advised him of his rights and then asked if he was aware the area was baited. He made a feeble attempt at denying any knowledge of the block initially but then rather quickly admitted he had placed the block there. I asked if he was aware he was hunting in a safety zone on the WMA. He explained he did know that, but he didn't feel the area should be a safety zone, and it was his property the safety zone was protecting, and therefore he didn't see why he couldn't hunt there. I explained the safety zone meant no hunting for anyone, and he was under arrest for that as well as hunting over bait.

I joined up with Hershel and wrote the fellow a couple of tickets. I asked if he understood the laws on baiting. Seeing how his private property was heavily baited and we were one week away from the opening day of the gun deer season, I wanted to be sure he knew what the law said. I explained how it was illegal to hunt in an area where feeding had taken place for ten days after all of the feed had been removed. I further stated many hunters were often confused and would tell us the bait had been put out over ten days ago. I wanted to be sure he understood this seeing how even if he immediately removed the bait from his private property, it would still be considered baited on opening day. He stated he totally understood the law and he apologized for placing the bait on the WMA. With that we were on our way back to our vehicle. Once we reached the car, I asked Hershel if he thought they would hunt the baited property next weekend and he replied, "Probably so."

During the next week we returned to the property. I was anxious to see if the landowner had made any attempt to clean up the feed. As stealthily as possible we eased into the property and checked the feeders. He had not made any effort to remove the bait and may have added to it. While in the area I observed three does easing through the property. I was on the north side of the property while Hershel was on the south side. I watched the deer as they traversed the property north to south. They were probably 100 yards from me as I eased along through the woods. The deer walked almost the entire length of the property and went directly to the corn pile Hershel was checking on the south side. This was interesting from the standpoint that hunters always asked us how

AGAIN?

far they had to be from bait not to be in violation while hunting. At that time, the law stated bait was anything that acted as an attractant to wildlife, and animals going to and from the bait could not be hunted. In this incidence, the deer entered the property at least 200 yards from the bait yet were still being attracted by it. That is why we always told the hunters there was no set distance they could be away from the bait. This changed many years later when regrettably folks were allowed to hunt by aid of bait as long as it was 100 yards from them and out of their line of sight by a natural barrier.

Saturday morning found us once again easing through the woods toward the baited stands. I must admit, after walking under the hunter the week before, I was much more cautious this time. This trip was somewhat easier in the fact we knew where the stands were. However, there was never a guarantee the hunters would use the permanent stands; therefore, you always had to be vigilant. There is no way of knowing how many hunters I have walked past in my career. By their good judgment and the grace of God I was able to keep walking. As I approached the first location, I spotted a hunter in the stand. Fortunately, he was facing away from me. I was able to get within about 30 yards of his location without being detected. That was as close as I wanted to be. I employed a technique I used many times: I whistled to get his attention. I learned early on it wasn't wise to startle someone holding a loaded firearm. As often was the case, my first whistle solicited no response. This always amazed me. Many times, I would have to repeatedly whistle and eventually yell at the hunters to get their attention. I whistled loudly and got this hunter's attention. He slowly turned around, and I recognized it was the same fellow from last week. Upon meeting my gaze, his jaw went slack, and he simply said, "Again!" I felt the same way. I told him to come down and again arrested him for hunting over bait. I escorted the man down to the next stand where Hershel was writing tickets for hunting over bait and hunting without wearing hunter orange. We finished writing the tickets and explained the bonds and were on our way.

The next month the subject appeared in court before the district judge. After pleading guilty to two counts of hunting over bait and to hunting in a safety zone, the defendant was given fines and costs totaling over $1,200. Included in his sentence was some advice from the judge. He told the man it was evident he had a propensity to hunt over bait, but he had better not do it AGAIN!

How many times has the Lord looked down on what we were doing or thinking and shook his head and said, "Again?" Think about it.

Sliding and Shooting
(Drama at the Skating Rink)

THE VEHICLE WAS STILL SLIDING when the first shot rang out. My first impression was we had caught another road hunter; however, when I saw my partner with his gun drawn and a man on his hands and knees on the ground, I knew there was more to it.

If I had to guess, I would say every officer probably has a favorite place to work. These are normally spots where we have had success. We often refer to these areas as honey holes. My honey hole was an old skating rink—or should I say an old skating rink site.

Like many places in rural Alabama all the locals would continue to refer to locations by what had been there twenty years ago or maybe who had owned the property thirty years ago. As a young wildlife biologist, I worked extensively with the two veteran game wardens in Coosa County. They each told me it was essential that I learn the whole county like the back of my hand. There I was thinking I had enough to do just learning the thirty-eight thousand acres comprising the Coosa WMA I was responsible for, and now these guys were telling me I also needed to learn the other six hundred square miles in the county. I remember well one summer day when I received a call from one of the seasoned wardens advising me of some illegal activity that needed to be investigated at the Hughes Fish Camp. Although I had been studying the county map I had to ask the officer how to get to the location. He said for me to go west on Highway 22 and turn right at Hull's old store and follow that road to the end. I barreled down the highway as fast as I thought I could while still spotting the old store that marked where I needed to turn. As I neared the river, which represented the county line, I knew I had not seen anything that resembled a store. I did not want to have to call the officer back and inform him I had missed my turn—not only because he would see how inept I was but also because at that time everyone in the state was on one radio frequency, and everyone within sixty or seventy miles would hear everything said. Knowing all this, I keyed the microphone and called the warden. I told him I had been up and down the road and somehow I had not seen the old store. He immediately replied that the store had burnt twenty years earlier. I instinctively called back and asked how I was supposed to know that. His long silence told me this was a conversation that would be better had face to face. That wouldn't be the last time I received directions like that. I digress.

The skating rink was no exception. The old roller-skating rink had been located in a sparsely populated area between the communities of Weogufka and Unity in west central Coosa County. I always found it interesting there had ever been a skating rink out in the middle of nowhere. However, wildlife biologist Gene Carver and I worked the area many times and were successful more often than not.

The skating rink site was almost perfect for working the deer decoy. Many people do not understand one of the most difficult aspects of working the decoy is finding a well-hidden vantage point from which to monitor the activity. The skating rink area provided both a good decoy position along an old logging road and a good hiding spot just across the paved road. In addition, the area was located along an open stretch of road where you could see at least a quarter of mile to the east and a couple of hundred yards to the west.

During the deer season, it was a rare thing for Gene and me to have a Saturday when we did not have a management area hunt to work. It was even rarer for both of us to have the same Saturday "off." When this did occur, we decided such a day would be a good time to give the skating rink location a try.

We arrived early in the morning, and, after hiding our trucks, we proceeded across the road with the decoy. This was always a somewhat dangerous part of the decoy detail. Walking around carrying a six-point buck on your shoulder during the hunting season in rural Alabama wasn't the wisest thing to do!

About as soon as we got the decoy put in place, the weather decided it didn't want to cooperate. Although a light rain is a good time to use the decoy, a heavy downpour is miserable to work in. We decided the rain was coming down a little too hard to try it, so we loaded the deer back into the truck. We had gone less than a mile down the road when, suddenly, the rain stopped. We decided to return and give it another shot.

We positioned the deer decoy in the old logging road approximately sixty yards from the paved county road. I usually liked to have the deer at least one hundred yards from the road during the day; however, this place had worked well in the past, and when something worked we tried to stay with it. We made sure the deer was working properly and started back across the road. While crossing the road, we heard the telltale roar of the tires of a four-wheel-drive vehicle approaching, and we ran to get out of the road. The vehicle was moving at a pretty good pace, and I barely made it to my truck before the vehicle reached our setup.

When the vehicle passed the decoy, the driver immediately locked up the brakes and began sliding down the wet road. The vehicle had barely come to a halt when a shot rang out. I jumped in the truck as Gene took off toward the road on foot. Within seconds a second shot sounded.

One of the exciting and dangerous aspects of working the decoy was you never knew how the shooter would react. While some would immediately speed off like their hair was on fire, others would either continue shooting or simply sit in the vehicle with a slack jaw, staring at the wonder deer.

As I charged over the hill and into the road, the first thing I saw was Gene with his gun drawn and a subject on the ground on his hands and knees. I pulled in behind the truck, and, seeing the driver still in the vehicle, I immediately made my way toward his side of the Ford Bronco. I advised the driver to place his hands on the steering wheel. He immediately complied. I opened the door and removed him and his Browning 25-06 lever-action rifle from the vehicle. Gene had holstered his pistol and retrieved a rifle from the ground beside the passenger. With the weapons safely in my vehicle we placed the individuals under arrest and began preparing bonds for hunting from the public road, hunting by aid of a vehicle, and hunting without a permit. After the subjects signed their bonds and once again explained this was their first time to do anything like this, they were on their way.

Gene and I checked the decoy and critiqued our handling of the incident. Gene explained how when he ran over the hill and into the road he had come face to face with the passenger, who had exited the vehicle with his rifle and was trying to move into a position to take a shot. Seeing the young man running at him with a rifle in hand, he had instinctively drawn his gun and ordered him to the ground.

A check of the decoy revealed the driver had hit the deer twice in the white patch on the neck. The fact the two bullet holes were nearly touching each other caused us to wonder if he had really never shot out of the window before!

During this time, the judge and I had decided it would be a good idea to include as part of the violator's sentence the requirement to successfully complete a hunter education course. In addition, at our discretion, we could require the violator to make a presentation to the group. I decided this would be a good test case, and we required the shooter to give a short presentation to the next class. He did a very good job. He explained how he had made a quick decision that was neither safe nor wise. He also explained not only did he have to pay a hefty fine and attend the course, but he also had to put up with the embarrassment of everyone knowing what he had done. He said this really hit home when his young son accompanied him to Walmart. Seeing a full-size deer target on display in the sporting goods section, the young boy ran and draped himself across the deer and yelled, "Don't shoot it, Daddy, don't shoot it!" I said to myself, this guy has probably been punished enough!

Sometimes life happens really fast. The guys in this story spotted what they thought was a deer standing on the side of the road and made what seemed to be a split-second decision to shoot it. In actuality, I would surmise the decision to shoot the deer was made way before they spotted it. That is true with many of our decisions. I once heard a quote that said, "Temptation often comes through a door that was intentionally left open."

We make choices every day of our lives. Our choices have consequences and not only for us. The Bible says, "Choose you this day whom you will serve." If you make the choice to follow Jesus as your Savior you have made a commitment that will affect all of your other choices. The Bible says the Lord will not tempt you: "There hath no temptation taken you but such as is common to man: but God is faithful, who will not suffer you to be tempted above that ye are able; but will with the temptation also make a way to escape, that ye may be able to bear it" (1 Corinthians 10:13).

I have a good Christian brother who is a reformed wildlife outlaw. He once told me he carries his turkey gun in his toolbox to help him avoid the temptation of shooting a turkey out the window of his vehicle, which he has done many times in the past. The temptation is still there; however, he is able to withstand it. The point isn't that he doesn't shoot from the window because he can't reach his gun; it is that as a follower of Christ he does not want to break the law. A change has been wrought in his life, and he wants to do his best to make choices that please God.

What about you? Who are you trying to please? What type of choices are you making? Who are your choices affecting? This case involved an adult and a minor. There is an adage that says we teach what we know, but we produce what we are. As stated earlier I have no doubt the plan to shoot any deer spotted was probably put in place as soon as they left home. What are you demonstrating to the children under your care and control by the choices you make, the words you say, and your actions? Think about it.

And the Cuffs Wouldn't Fit!

WORKING DEER HUNTS on the wildlife management area (WMA) was an every-weekend occurrence during the deer season for my first seventeen years with game and fish. Working at the check station was a time-consuming endeavor and ranged from painfully boring to extremely hectic. For many years hunters were required to present their licenses and obtain a permit on the day of the hunt. Our permits indicated the check station would open no later than 5:00 a.m. Since our area was quite large (38,000 acres) and took a while to traverse, we would normally open by 4:30 a.m. to accommodate the early birds who had a long drive to reach their hunting destination. We normally closed the check station around 6:30 p.m.

Doing this for two days could really eat into our forty-hour work week. During the early years on the WMA it wasn't uncommon to have in excess of one thousand hunters on some hunts. Therefore, we were often greeted with a long line when we arrived. On special hunts, such as our either-sex drawing hunt, we would try to arrive even earlier to handle the crowd that sometimes reached fifteen hundred. One of these mornings proved to be quite memorable.

I had long suspected we had some illegal hunting taking place in the wee hours of the morning prior to the hunt so, I decided I would leave my house around 3:00 a.m. and see if I couldn't locate some of the evildoers. Everything went as planned as far as leaving the house goes; however, my plans were soon dismantled. The WMA was approximately fifteen miles from my home, which was two miles east of the town of Rockford. Alabama Highway 22 would take me halfway, and County Road 29 led to the checking station.

Although Rockford is the county seat, when the entire county has a population of eleven thousand, you can imagine not much was happening as I rolled through town at 3:05 a.m. However, that all changed when I rounded a curve about a mile west of town and observed a pickup truck stopped in the road. As I slowly approached the vehicle, I could not see anyone inside the cab. My first thought was someone had shot a deer, and they were out trying to retrieve it. This illegal activity was very prevalent. As I eased past the truck, I scanned the wood line along the side of the road but saw no one. I picked up the radio microphone and called the county jail, waking up the dispatcher. I turned around and pulled up behind the vehicle and gave the tag number to the radio operator. Although I knew there were no other officers on duty in the entire county, I at least wanted the dispatcher to know where I was. I activated my blue lights and exited the truck.

Not knowing the whereabouts of a possible night hunter who was likely armed is an uneasy feeling. I cautiously made my way to the truck, hoping the gun might have been left inside. What I found provided some relief—but only briefly. While approaching I had noticed the brake lights appeared to be on, and once I arrived at the cab I understood why. Lying in the front seat was a large man. I noticed the truck gearshift was in drive and the man's foot was on the brake. I also noticed the man appeared to be DEAD!

And the Cuffs Wouldn't Fit!

I tried the door and found it was locked. Banging on the window received no response. I moved to the passenger side of the truck and found the door unlocked. As I opened the door, I received a clue as to what the situation was when the smell of alcoholic beverage slapped me in the face. Now I at least had the hope the man was only drunk and not dead. I began trying to wake the man by yelling, which was really loud inside the truck, but got no response. Finally, I reached over and began to shake the guy and after several hard shakes, I heard a grunt. I was glad to hear it.

I was eventually able to get the man roused up. I reached over and put the truck in park and told the man to unlock his door. I hurried around to the driver's side door and opened it. "What are you doing?" I asked, and I must admit I was surprised when he replied he was delivering a load of wood. When I replied, "You don't *have* a load of wood," the fellow snapped his head around and said, "Well I *had* a load of wood!" I am not making that up.

I ordered him to get out of the truck, and it was at this point I realized he was much larger than I had first thought. More than once in my career I had told someone to get out of their vehicle and then sort of wished I hadn't. This guy was big; however, he was still pretty much out of it. I helped him to the rear of the truck and told him to put his hands on the tailgate. Even in a drunken stupor, a fellow this size would be a handful if he suddenly decided he didn't want to comply. I had witnessed that type of immediate mood change many times dealing with intoxicated individuals, and I didn't want to take a chance at 3:15 a.m. in the middle of nowhere and with no possibility of backup.

I pulled his right hand around behind his back, and it was at this inopportune time I made an interesting discovery. Handcuffs are **NOT** one size fits all! As I attempted to apply the cuff to the big man's wrist, I realized the wrist was bigger than the cuff.

Never having had this occur, I wasn't exactly sure what to do next. I distinctly remember thinking it would have been nice if they would have covered this at the police academy. I grabbed the cuff and squeezed it hard onto his wrist and finally heard it click. I quickly grabbed the other wrist and went through the same procedure. The man said, "That hurts my hands," and I assured him I would remove them as soon as we reached the jail. The last thing I wanted was an intoxicated man in the front seat with me with his hands free. I placed the man in my truck, moved his truck out of the road, and we made a speedy trip to the county jail. While en route, I called the dispatcher and told them I would need someone to administer a Breathalyzer test. Shortly after I arrived, Rockford Police Chief Mike Arms showed up, looking like most people summoned out of bed at 3:30 in the morning look. Mike told the subject to follow him to the Intoxilyzer room, and the subject replied, "I ain't taking that test." A check of his driver's history revealed this was his fifth DUI.

The case came to court the next month, and the defendant was found guilty, lost his driver's license, and paid a fine and court costs. He later went to prison for drug trafficking. Although I never dealt with him again, I did have an encounter with his sister a few years later. That's another interesting story.

While preparing this book for publication, I was working patrol with Coosa County Sheriff's Deputy Mike Rudd when we made a traffic stop on a suspected drunk driver. As I spoke with the suspect I ascertained his name and realized it was the same as the man in this story. I asked if he knew the man, and he looked at me and replied, "That's my daddy." As we were placing the man in the patrol car for DUI, I told the deputy I arrested the suspect's dad for the same thing over twenty-five years ago. We teach what we know, but we reproduce what we are. Think about it.

Brigetta's Dibble
(God at Work)

As a wildlife biologist and conservation enforcement officer I met a lot of people including many agency personnel. Being a law enforcement officer permeates all aspects of your life. I realized early on that I made a quick assessment or "read" of everyone I met be it a landowner, agency employee or someone at church. It became and remains automatic. I have often said this is both a blessing and a curse. A blessing in that your "read" often allows you to keep your guard up, a curse in that you often realize many people aren't who they claim or try to persuade you they are. The adage, what you are speaks so loudly I can't hear what you say, comes to mind.

Working in natural resources you quickly realize the vast majority of employees are men. I don't know the percentage but I'm sure it's high. This is changing. When I began my career in Game & Fish we had no female biologists or game wardens. This changed rather quickly as we began hiring women in both sections. However, even today females comprise maybe 10% of the department.

While female natural resource professionals were rare with us, they were even more scarce in the forestry field. Therefore, I was a little surprised when I met Brigetta Giles, a forester with the Alabama Forestry Commission (AFC). My quick "read" of Brigetta was a good one. I found her to be a conscientious consummate professional. She was dedicated to her employer and profession. It was blatantly obvious she had a heart for natural resources and for serving the public. It was very refreshing. And it was always that way.

Although we didn't work together on a very regular basis, our paths crossed from time to time as I worked with the TREASURE Forest program across the state. The TREASURE Forest program recognized landowners who were doing an exceptional job of managing their forest property for multiple use. It normally required a property visit from both a forester and wildlife biologist who provided recommendations to help the landowners achieve the goals they selected. My Coosa County AFC Forester, Blake Kelley, and I had wholeheartedly embraced the TREASURE Forest program and through hard work and with a great group of dedicated landowners we were able to see more properties certified as TREASURE Forests than any other county in the state. During this time, my familiarity and zeal for the program landed me on the statewide TREASURE Forest committee which I chaired for several years.

Through the years we conducted numerous trainings across the state in attempts to educate and motivate resource professionals charged to work with the program. These trainings often lasted all day. In order to keep folks engaged and to get them back after lunch or breaks, we would give away some door prizes. It was on one of these occasions that I received an even deeper insight into Brigetta.

Door prizes for a group of natural resource professionals usually were different than what most folks are used to. We might give away a compass or a work vest or a field guide for birds or plants. At an Alabama Natural Resource Council training in May of 2008 one of the prizes was a tree planting dibble. I'm sure

Brigetta's Dibble

everyone is familiar with a dibble, but just in case let me explain what it is. Simply put a dibble is a piece of steel approximately three feet long with a handle on one end and a beveled edge on the other. The beveled edge of the dibble is forced into the ground making a small slit in the earth. The slit is just large enough that a bare root pine seedling can be placed in it. This scenario of tree planting is carried out millions of times each year across the country. I hope my description makes you think it's a lot of hard back breaking work because it is.

Each county AFC office normally had a dibble, if nothing else for demonstration purposes although several offices loaned their dibble out from time to time to folks who had a few trees to plant. Those who had a lot of acres to plant hired crews who were used to doing the back-breaking work and were exceptionally good at it. It was amazing to watch one of these crews move across the landscape. During my tenure the majority of these crews were made up of people from Honduras and Guatemala. These folks would normally carry two bags full of trees attached to their belt. When they exhausted their supply of trees, they would run back to the truck and resupply. These workers were normally paid per tree planted. It was not unusual to have a good planter who would plant 1500 or more trees each day! It was amazing to watch and I did not envy them.

The name drawn for the dibble door prize was Brigetta Giles. While most people are somewhat happy to win any door prize, that wasn't the case with Brigetta. She wasn't only happy, she was elated. So much so I got the feeling there had to be more to her joy than just winning a simple dibble. I was right.

I asked Brigetta why she was so excited and she told the following story. When she was preparing to go to college in Auburn, she applied for and received a scholarship given in honor of a man's son who had been killed. Ironically, the man who had provided the scholarship had recently come by her office and told her he needed a dibble. As I had mentioned it wasn't unusual for a landowner to borrow a dibble if they had a small planting job, however that wasn't why he needed it. He explained his other son was now serving as a covert missionary in a foreign country. He was assisting the people with his forestry expertise and while doing so he would witness to them when the opportunity presented itself. The son had contacted his father advising he needed a tree planting dibble. Although she knew she would have to replace it, Brigetta said she could not turn down the man's request and gave him the only dibble she had. She explained she had told the rangers in her county she would replace it and now she could!

I have often used the adage, where God guides He provides. I have seen it happen numerous times. God continues to see that his work gets done and those that do it get blessed. Praise His name.

As of this writing, Brigetta has moved up through the ranks and now serves as the first ever female Regional Forester for the AFC. She's a true asset to the department and people of Alabama and I'm very proud of her accomplishments and that I can call her my friend and colleague. I had her pegged as a winner from the start and I was right!

Not A Nice Person

I LEARNED EARLY IN MY CAREER many of the folks I would deal with wouldn't be nice people, but they didn't have to be totally rude, crude, and socially unacceptable just because they were caught. I always attempted to treat people as well as they would let me. Surprisingly some of them didn't appreciate that!

My dinner table chair alarm was working flawlessly. Just as my rear end hit the seat, the phone rang. It was my fellow officer, CEO Hershel Patterson. He advised he had just received a call from the president of Bama Hunting Association (BHA), a local hunting club, who had reported someone had shot a deer from the road on their property. He said he would soon be en route; however, since I was twenty miles closer, I should probably start that way. Within minutes I was barreling south down US Highway 231 to the Elmore/Coosa County line.

I was very familiar with BHA and probably not in the way you might suppose. The president of the club was a retired air force lieutenant colonel. He was a no-nonsense, get-the-job-done type. Although he was originally from Wisconsin, he had been in Montgomery for many years, and it was obvious he had no plans to go back north. (Some folks in the South have a description for Yankees who fit in that category.) He had graciously offered me a membership in the hunting club. As one might imagine we had to be very particular about our hunting activity. Many folks were of the opinion that we hunted wherever we wanted, and no one was going to do anything about it. The opposite was the truth. Although we often received offers to hunt on properties, we had to know the landowner very well and trust them before we would accept the invitation. Dealing with what we dealt with on a daily basis, trust did not come easily. I had never had any reason to distrust the BHA president, and therefore I became a member of the club for a few years. Unfortunately, the countless hours we worked during the deer season left such little time to hunt that it wasn't worth the annual dues. Nevertheless, my previous membership and corresponding knowledge of the property gave me a great advantage when it came to working the club.

A large portion of the property was literally on the county line, and I had to go into neighboring Elmore County and come back north to access the parcel where the illegal hunting had supposedly taken place.

Arriving in the area, I was traveling pretty fast down the dirt road when a hunter flagged me down. The middle-aged man identified himself as a member of the club and introduced me to his son. The boy was your typical gangly fifteen-year-old and was taller than both me and his dad. The father told his son to tell me what had happened. The young man explained he had been in a tree stand when he observed a black pickup truck coming down the road at approximately 3:00 p.m. The truck passed by his location and returned, going in the opposite direction, about ten minutes later. At about 5:30, which was about fifteen minutes after good dark, the vehicle returned, moving slowly along the road. As he watched from his lofty perch, the truck stopped in the road. The driver stealthily opened his door, triggering the overhead light, which illuminated the interior of the truck. The young hunter observed the outlaw as he placed his rifle between the door and the cab and shot. Immediately after the shot, the woods erupted as a deer came crashing through and piled up just past the young hunter's stand. With that, the shooter casually closed the door and drove off.

Upon hearing the late shot, the father, who was en route to retrieve his son, hurried on to the tree. When he arrived at the stand his son excitedly told what had just occurred. As the son climbed down, the father found the deer, a five-point buck. The pair dragged the deer out of the woods and loaded it in their truck and called the club president, who in turn had phoned Hershel.

The young hunter stated after they had returned to their vehicle, he recognized the guttural growl of the shooter's truck returning. The driver pulled up to where he had shot earlier, and two occupants got out and headed into the woods, and they were still down there.

Armed with an eyewitness the shooter obviously didn't know existed, I hurried down to the subject's truck. I could see two flashlight beams in the woods as I exited my vehicle. I must admit it, I found it humorously ironic when one of the subjects hollered at me saying, "Don't shoot, there's people down here."

My response of "What are y'all doing down there?" was met by a somewhat belligerent "Who wants to know?" To which I replied, "The state game warden—now come on up here."

Not receiving an immediate response and not wanting to give the subjects an opportunity to get their stories straight, I started down into the woods. I once again asked what they were doing, and one subject replied, "We are tracking a deer." I told him to mark his spot and come with me.

By this time, I was shining the beam of my Maglite in the subject's face. It was easy to see he wasn't happy to see me, and he didn't appear to think I was a nice person. After returning to the truck, it was quickly apparent which subject was the offender.

His belligerent spontaneous exclamation, "I shot that deer on our land," spoke volumes to me. As did his snarling demeanor. I told him that was the type information I needed, but first I needed to advise them of their rights. As he huffed I read them the Miranda warning, and they each stated they understood. I asked the quieter, less belligerent subject to step to the rear of my vehicle while I questioned his partner. The look on his face said he would rather not be associated with his loud-mouthed counterpart.

I returned to the mouthy subject and requested his ID and asked if he had permission to be on the property where he was tracking the deer. He said he did not, but he was trying to retrieve a deer he had shot on his hunting club, and it had run across the line. I asked him to tell me what had occurred that day, beginning at 1:00 p.m. I had found it was normally a good technique to ask a subject to tell me what had occurred beginning much earlier in the day. Most defendants, especially the guilty ones, would have already formulated their story about what had just occurred, and asking them about something many hours earlier normally worked to throw them off their game.

The fellow said he and his buddy had decided to go hunting. He had brought his buddy over and dropped him off at a stand while he went to another tract of land to hunt. While stalking he had jumped a buck and shot it. I asked how big the deer was, and he replied he wasn't sure. He went on to say he knew it was a buck. "We shoot bucks, we ain't like this club," he said, referring to the fact that BHA had been under the state deer management program since its inception and harvested antlerless deer and large bucks while passing small young bucks. "Tell me how you came to this spot," I asked. He said he had lost the blood trail in the woods. However, as he came to pick up his buddy, he spotted the blood going across the road and got back on the trail. I told him it was amazing to me how he could see a blood trail (which was actually three or four drops of blood on the edge of the road where the deer had been shot) while driving down the road. He replied "I did" in a matter-of-fact tone I'm sure he felt emphasized he was telling the truth but to me did just the opposite.

I decided it was time to hear what the passenger had to say. I told the subject to stay where he was while I went to talk with his counterpart. I approached the man and asked him to tell me what had occurred this evening. His reply was, "Evidently more than I know about." That comment told me this fellow didn't want any part of what he sensed was going on. He stated the driver had dropped him off, came back after dark to get him, and had told him he had shot a buck. I asked if he had heard a shot while he was waiting to be picked up. He hesitated momentarily and disgustedly said he had heard a shot about five minutes before his friend came to get him. I asked him if it was dark when he heard the shot, and he replied it was. He said he did not know for sure what was going on, but it was obviously more than he wanted to be involved in. I asked if it would surprise him to know his hunting partner had stopped and shot a deer from the truck. Watching his face, I wasn't sure whether he was going to throw up or answer. "No" was all he said.

I returned to the hostile poacher and told him I was now ready to hear the truth. In a not-so-nice tone he told me he had already told me the truth. I stated I was having some trouble believing his story, especially since his version was so much different than the one I had gotten from the other fellow. The subject quickly pointed out that his partner had not been hunting with him. It was time to drop the hammer. I wish I had a picture of his face when I said his hunting partner wasn't the guy I was talking about. He wanted to refute what I had just said, but he obviously didn't have the foggiest idea what I was talking about. I let that hang in the air for a few seconds and said, "I'm talking about the guy who watched you stop and shoot the deer!" This took him back somewhat, but he quickly recovered and stated he had shot the deer on his hunting club. I countered by telling him he had shot the deer from his truck right where we were now standing. He again huffed and puffed and shook his head. I asked, "If that's not the case then how is it I have the deer in the back of my truck?"

This little nugget took him totally by surprise and solicited exactly what I wanted. He did not deny shooting it; instead, he excitedly asked, "How big is it?"

Think about it. If I had stopped you and accused you of illegally shooting a deer, at night, from the road, from your vehicle, and on a property where you did not have permission and you had not done any of that, would you give a rip how big the deer was? I didn't think so.

I told the outlaw how big it was didn't really matter since it didn't belong to him. He asked me how I knew it was the deer he had shot, and I responded I knew because it was the deer that had run through the woods and crashed right under the guy who watched him shoot it! Although the fellow kept the indignant scowl on his face, the look in his eyes said he realized his private part had just got caught in his zipper! Totally frustrated he told me I couldn't prove anything. I informed him we would see who could prove what in district court, where he would be facing charges of hunting at night, hunting without a permit, hunting from a public road, and hunting by the aid of a vehicle. After completing the necessary paperwork, I told him he was free to go, and I looked forward to seeing him in court. Based on his body language and what I considered to be honest candid answers, I did not charge the passenger with anything.

The next month in Coosa County district court the cases were called, and the defendant and I approached the judge's bench. The defendant had a scowl on his face that said he was ready to fight these trumped-up charges. Unfortunately for him, he did not know that Judge Bobby Teel quickly chewed up and spit out people like him on a regular basis. The judge advised him of the charges and asked how he pled, to which he gruffly responded, "Not guilty." While I was sure the violator didn't pick up on the subtle change in the judge's breathing, I definitely did, and I knew he would eventually. The judge instructed us to raise our right hand and be sworn in. The judge looked at me and asked why I brought these charges against the defendant.

I responded the charges were the result of an investigation, and I would like for him to hear from an eyewitness to the incident. I motioned for the young hunter to come forward. I introduced him to the judge, who swore him in and asked him to tell what had occurred. He provided the details of the case up until I arrived on the scene. I testified to what had occurred, including a couple of comments concerning the defendant's demeanor and his aversion to telling the truth. Although again not visible to everyone, I could tell the judge was highly perturbed. Fortunately, for the good guys, it was not unusual for the judge to get extremely upset with game law violators. This day was no exception. The judge immediately began writing out the disposition of the case.

When the defendant saw the judge had already written *guilty* on the case action summary, he blurted out, "You didn't even let me speak."

The judge stopped writing, literally threw down his pen, glared at the defendant, and through clenched teeth hissed, "What do you want to say?"

The now-shaken defendant stammered around and said, "I didn't do this."

With that the judge picked up his pen and resumed writing. He looked at the defendant and said, once again through clenched teeth, "I don't think you're a very nice person." He informed the violator the court had found him guilty as charged, and he was to pay fines and courts costs totaling $2,436, and he would serve 240 days in jail. It was not at all unusual for the judge to give jail time in this type of case; however, it was normally always suspended on payment of fine and costs. That wasn't the deal in this case. The judge advised the defendant he was in the custody of the sheriff. A deputy escorted him to the jury box where, with a dazed look on his face, he sat with the other criminals.

During a court recess, I was approached by the ADA, who wanted to know why the judge had given the subject the jail time "to serve." I told him he would have to ask the judge, but I guessed it was because he wasn't a nice person. Not impressed, the ADA stated he saw no reason why this man should sit in jail for eight months when our jail was already overcrowded. He went on to say this would surely lead to an appeal that would just cost the taxpayers more money. I knew this was code for "I'm going to get the jail time dropped." I often wondered whose side this guy was on! Taking the obvious hint, I asked if he wanted me to see if the defendant would like to pay off the fines and costs if we could suspend the jail time. He indicated he thought that was a good idea.

I approached the defendant, who was still sitting in the jury box. I asked what he planned to do, and he emphatically responded he was going to appeal the case. He growled, "I'm not going to jail for something I'm not guilty of."

I hesitated and said I could understand that. I did my best to look as if I was in deep thought about the situation as the scowling man studied me. After about thirty seconds I told him I was prepared to offer to drop the jail time if he wanted to pay the fines and costs, but I didn't want him to do that if he wasn't guilty.

"I'll do it," he almost yelled.

"No, I don't want you to do that if you aren't guilty," I repeated.

"I'm guilty," he said.

"But I thought you were innocent," I said.

"I'm guilty and I'll pay it," he said.

I looked at him as if contemplating whether or not to allow him to pay it off, as if it was up to me! I thought, "My how quickly one can have a change of heart." I again asked the once-cocky, now-groveling defendant, "Are you sure?"

"I'm sure," was his quick reply.

I said, "Okay," and the defendant immediately motioned for a friend to come to him and told him to go to the bank and get $2,500 and get back as soon as possible. He thanked me for dropping the jail time. I told him, "Hey, I'm a nice person!"

Just like this guy, you probably don't like the feeling when you know you're caught. Well, guess what, you're caught. The eyes of the Lord are in every place seeing ALL we do. Yet, even though He knows it all, He still died in our place to save us from our sin. If you don't know Him and the full pardon of sin He offers, today is the day to change that.

Moment of Decision

YOU WOULD THINK someone looking at the business end of a pistol from a distance of about two feet would quickly comply with what the officer holding the gun was telling them. When they didn't, it made for an extremely intense and stressful situation.

There are two ways to consistently make good cases. Work hard and long and/or receive good information. There is no substitute for hard work; however, one good tip can sure make things easier for an officer. There are many different types of informants conservation enforcement officers work with. The word *informant* often carries a connotation of something underhanded or deceitful. This should not be the case. I think you can consider anyone who gives you information as an informant; however, one thing that does need to be understood is the motivation of an informant.

It is easy to understand the motivation of a landowner who tells you about a problem occurring on their property or a hunter who realizes, unlike most, violators are stealing from him, the legitimate sportsman. These people have a stake in the wildlife on the property. In many cases they may have thousands of dollars invested in it! No one appreciates someone violating their space and basically stealing from them. As a matter of fact, toward the end of my career I began to see landowners suing individuals who were caught hunting on their property without permission.

MOMENT OF DECISION

Another informant is the wildlife outlaws themselves. Many times, I have had a well-known violator supply me with information. Their information is normally always good. You need to try to understand their motivation. Normally they have for some reason become angry with another violator, they want to reduce competition, they want to divert attention from their own nefarious activities, or they are in hopes of favorable treatment down the road. Many times, an apprehended violator wants to plea bargain with some information. It is probably not advisable to ever really trust these individuals; however, their information is normally very good and beneficial.

Another type of informant is someone who is simply "in the know" yet despises the outlaw activity and therefore supplies you with the information. I had a fellow who was in this category and was an excellent source of information. His reports almost always panned out and resulted in numerous arrests and thousands of dollars in fines. As a former law enforcement officer, he knew the type of information we needed and did a great job supplying it. I was introduced to the man by my partner, Hershel Patterson. Due to Hershel's endorsement, I never doubted the fellow; however, an incident would occur that gave me an opportunity to see his true colors.

Having received numerous complaints of hunting from the road, fellow wildlife biologist Gene Carver and I decided to set up a decoy detail in a location that had always been our honey hole. The area was in a sparsely populated part of the county. It was one of those rare places that had both a good place to set the decoy and a good hiding place from which to observe it in close juxtaposition to each other. There once had been an old roller-skating rink on the property, and everyone knew the place as "the skating rink." Like many places in the rural South, the name hung on long after any evidence of the structure was present.

Gene and I had set the deer up in an old logging road about sixty yards off the county road. We normally liked to put the deer farther off the road in the daytime; however, this area had always worked well, and we stayed with it. Gene was stationed at the truck and I was hidden in the wood line across the road from the deer.

It wasn't long until I heard and then saw a green Ford pickup approaching our location. I noted two white males occupied the vehicle as it slowly moved past the deer. I wasn't sure whether or not they had seen the decoy as they continued down the road. Another advantage of this area was we could see the road for at least a quarter of a mile to the east. I continued to watch the vehicle and realized they were slowing down and then turning around. A driver's response to seeing the deer often allowed me to differentiate between experienced road hunters and amateurs. Your amateur road hunters would often slam on the brakes and immediately shoot the deer while the more experienced folks would simply ease off of the gas and coast on by as not to scare the deer away. Of course, this also had to do with which side of the road the deer was on and whether or not there was a passenger in the truck to do the shooting.

I watched as the truck slowly came back toward the deer and then slowly drove on past. You always worried that with multiple looks the violators would somehow realize the deer wasn't real. Luckily, being able to make the robotic head of the deer follow the vehicle as it went by often fooled folks. Within a minute the vehicle was once again coming toward the deer. This time the driver eased to a stop in the road, and I observed the passenger, a right-handed shooter, as he turned around in the seat so he could shoot. The passenger stuck the rifle out the window and BOOM! I left the cover of the woods and headed toward the truck on foot. BOOM! The shooter unleashed another round at the unmoving animal. Although the driver noticed the big game warden running toward him, he evidently didn't share it with the passenger, who shot for the third time. As I approached the truck, out of the corner of my eye I could see Gene coming over the hill in the green game and fish truck with the blue lights flashing. I yelled at the driver to raise his hands; however, his response was just the opposite in that he appeared to reach into the floorboard or under the seat.

Looking directly in his face from three feet away it appeared to me the man was at the moment of decision. This act prompted me to respond by drawing my .40-caliber pistol and leveling it at his head. Looking at the business end of the handgun at a distance of a less than two feet, he contemplated his next move a little longer than I thought it should take, but he eventually decided to comply and slowly raised his hands over his head. Gene came up and took the rifle from the passenger. I opened the driver's door and told him to exit and move to the rear of the vehicle. Once he was secured, I returned to the cab of the truck to see what, if anything, he had been reaching for. I slid my hand under the seat and felt the grip of what turned out to be a fully loaded 9mm pistol! What had been going through his mind I do not know; however, I knew what nearly went through it! I was thankful I had trusted my instincts and let him know I meant business by tapping my barrel on his window.

We gathered the necessary information and began the paperwork. As we stood on the side of the road, it was all I could do to keep from laughing when a carload of guys drove by and our shooter exclaimed, "Well if we hadn't of shot it, they would have!" We allowed them to sign their bonds and leave, less their rifle and pistol.

Gene and I went over and examined the deer and were amazed to find the fellow had missed it with all three shots. We decided to call it a day at the skating rink location and loaded the deer in the truck. One thing you didn't want to do was wear out a good decoy spot!

A few days later I once again received a call from my informant, who had some information for me. He gave me the info and then asked, "Do you think the judge will allow my son to pay the fines for shooting the decoy?"

I told him that would be my recommendation, but it would be the judge's call. He went on to say his son had come home and told him about the incident, saying, "Daddy, that deer looked so good, you'd a shot it too."

He said he responded, "No I would not."

We never mentioned the incident again. His son came to court and was allowed to pay the fines without receiving any jail time. The man continued to be a good source of information I could count on, and I did for the remainder of my career.

Law enforcement officers, especially wildlife officers, will likely never know how many times we have been the benefactor of someone else's good decision. That is likely true with you as well. Right now is probably a good time to praise God for it! Could this be your moment of decision? If you haven't chosen Jesus as your Savior, now is the time.

Like Sausage Through a Grinder

I LEARNED A LOT OF LESSONS during my career. One I learned early on was it made a real difference how you treated people. When you are tasked with policing people's recreation you are not their favorite person. This was definitely true of folks hunting but was probably more of a problem with recreational users of the WMA. The Coosa WMA consisted of 38,000 acres. It had over two hundred miles of dirt roads that were evidently perfect for riding and drinking beer or smoking a little dope. It had three primitive campgrounds, two of which would definitely qualify as in the middle of nowhere. There were two major creeks that ran through the area with several access points. In addition, there were two public boat launch areas. If you want to know what attracts outdoor-oriented folks to an area, I can tell you, it's water. Whether it was the desire to fish, swim, wade, skip rocks, or just sit around and drink, along the creek was the quintessential spot.

One of the public boat launch areas that was an ongoing headache for me wasn't actually on the WMA but was adjacent to it. While WMA regulations did not apply on the launch site, there was a long list of public launch regulations that were applicable. The prohibited activities included no fires, no camping, no firearms, no all-terrain vehicles, no littering, no picnicking unless tables were provided, and no loitering, just to name a few. The launch area was there to serve the boating public by allowing them an opportunity to launch their boat, and that was pretty much it. Of course, of all the things I observed happening on the launch areas, the launching of boats was probably the rarest! As a matter of fact, the launch on the area that gave me the most trouble was actually covered with silt to the point you could not launch a boat off of a trailer there. That being the case, the area quickly became party central and quite the headache. It wasn't that those partying at the area caused a tremendous amount of trouble, although I did respond to various fights, stabbings, and other serious incidents, but the headache was the property generated numerous complaints that had to be addressed.

One cool fall afternoon, I received a call stating there was a huge party going on at the launch. I dutifully got into my uniform and headed down to check things out. Another lesson I had learned was that reports of illegal activity were often highly exaggerated. I guess folks thought if they made it sound really significant they would get a better response, and that was maybe true to an extent. It often turned out that a "huge" crowd was four or five folks, and although the caller would report folks were shooting multiple times every night, I might stay in the area for a week and not hear a single shot. However, it turned out this caller was extremely accurate.

The launch was actually nothing more than a large parking lot approximately 150 yards long and 50 yards wide located adjacent to a 30- to 50-yard-wide strip of grass and trees alongside Hatchet Creek, a major creek that traversed the entire county. It was approximately 400 yards from and out of sight of the public road. As I eased along the entrance road dodging the potholes I noted it appeared there had been a lot of traffic into the area. When I rounded the corner into the parking lot I was shocked at what I saw. My quick estimate was there were probably fifty to sixty vehicles and over a hundred people on the site. I must admit I was taken aback by the size of the crowd, as it was much larger than I had ever seen there before. There was a huge bonfire blazing, and several coolers were evident. I realized it was more than I would be able to handle by myself.

While deciding what to do next, I noticed a vehicle coming at me at a high rate of speed. I wasn't sure what the driver was thinking, but it was obvious he was operating recklessly as he flew by me heading out of the area. I followed the car out of the area with the idea I would stop it and see if I could find out what was going on. This soon turned out to be a little more difficult than I had figured. When I got back to the public road, the vehicle was already out of sight. Since I could see farther to the south than to the north, I assumed the driver had gone north, and I headed in that direction. I grabbed the radio microphone and called the Coosa County SO. I informed the dispatcher I had a large contingent of people at the public launch, and I was going to need some assistance in dealing with it. I also advised I was currently in pursuit of a small white car northbound on County Road 29.

Eventually I gained sight of the car I was pursuing and went into full pursuit mode with lights and siren. County Road 29 was about as straight as a corkscrew, and driving it at seventy-plus miles per hour was not a treat. I ended up chasing the vehicle for almost four miles. The driver, a sixteen-year-old kid, finally stopped near Mt. Moriah Church. I approached the vehicle and requested a license from the driver. I asked why he was driving in such a reckless and dangerous manner, and he said he was in a hurry. I learned that many folks were really good at giving blatantly obvious and often stupid answers when confronted by law enforcement. I went back to my truck and called his license number in to dispatch. While waiting for a reply, a deputy called dispatch, saying he was at the launch and needed assistance. I could tell by the sound of his voice he was distressed. I hurriedly returned the driver's license and told him to slow down and I would be in touch with him. I ran back to my truck and once again quickly drove the corkscrew road back to the launch.

While I had been shocked when I pulled into the launch earlier, this time I was dumbfounded. As I rounded the corner in the failing light, there stood a deputy holding a shotgun on about a hundred people who were standing in the glow of the headlights of his car. I pulled up beside his car and exited my truck. He told me he had ordered everyone to stand in front of his vehicle until help arrived, and everyone had complied except for the folks at the fire. I told him to keep an eye on those in front of the car, and I would go and check the ones at the fire.

As I cautiously approached the fire I observed an individual adding wood to it. I advised him it was illegal to tend a fire on the launch area. He replied, "I didn't start it," and I replied that he was tending it. I asked for his driver's license. He was a big, stocky guy with a scowl on his face and his attitude. This type of situation had the great potential to spiral out of control in a heartbeat. There was a very fine line between letting him understand I meant business and not embarrassing him in front of his peers to the point that our confrontation escalated.

As he stood and stared at me I again asked for his identification. I was well aware every eye was on us. I also knew the deputy and I were highly outnumbered and probably highly outgunned if I didn't miss my guess. It was a tense moment. What was I going to do if he refused to cooperate? It was obvious several of the folks in the crowd were intoxicated, and the murmuring was growing louder. I knew if the crowd got behind this guy, coaxing him to resist me, things could go south really fast. It was time to either back off or make a stand. While I had experienced many heated confrontations, I had never been in a situation just like this.

As I stood waiting on a response from the fire guy, I noticed a truck near the fire had firewood in the back of it. I surmised whoever owned the truck was likely responsible for the fire. I asked, "Whose truck is this?"

Nobody said anything for a minute, and then the fire-tending guy said, "It's mine."

Fortunately, this revelation changed the situation. I gave the guy my best "you know you're guilty" look, and in a somewhat joking tone asked, "Now whose fire, is it?"

"It's mine," was his now somewhat sheepish reply.

I found over the years when folks know they are caught their demeanor often changes. I was very thankful this was one of those times. I again asked for his driver's license and he handed it to me. I told him I would get back with him. Having broken the ice, so to speak, I attempted to get everyone's attention. I told them I needed everyone to go to their vehicles and wait on us to come to them. This was taking a risk, seeing how I was sure several of the vehicles held weapons; however, I thought it would be better to get the people into small groups than into a huge mass. I returned to the deputy and told him we needed to find a sober driver for each group and send them on their way. He agreed, and we started the long process.

Things went relatively smoothly, with the exception that some of the more intoxicated folks were feeling no pain and had lost their better judgment. After we cuffed a couple of them and placed them in the back of the deputy's car, the others calmed down. At the end of the night we had finally arranged for safe rides for everyone. We had released those who had been detained to their sober friends, and now I was left with only the fire guy. I explained to him he was in violation of several rules of the area, and his truck loaded with firewood proved his intent to violate the rule of no fires. I explained I had waited until everyone was gone so as not to embarrass him in front of his friends but that I was issuing him a ticket for the fire. Although he wasn't happy about it he did shake my hand. He paid the fine and court costs prior to court. I did follow up with the sixteen-year-old driver whom I had chased up the road and wrote him a reckless driving ticket.

Fast forward a few years. I had evidently decided that working game and fish law enforcement wasn't dangerous enough, so I had volunteered to serve as an umpire for Little League baseball. Oh, my goodness. If you want to know how folks really feel about you, call their child or worse yet their grandchild out on a close play at home plate! I had just thought people didn't like the game warden. However, when I thought about it, it was much the same. I was once again policing people's recreation. While the kids were rarely a problem, the parents were a much different story!

At the end of each season our Little League would host a regional tournament. I only thought the regular season was bad. Oh boy. For many years I was the umpire in chief and called most of the games behind the plate. Prior to each game we would hold a conference at the plate, which included managers, coaches, and the umpires. Usually our tournament dates would coincide with the southeastern conference tournament, which was held in Hoover, Alabama, about seventy miles up the road from us.

During one plate conference, I came up with an idea I continued to use for several years. After we assembled and shook hands I asked the coaches and managers if they had been keeping up with the tournament, and they all stated they had, and I said, "Well this isn't it." I continued, saying, "These are little kids trying to learn how to play baseball." I told them I expected them to act like a coach who was trying to train young boys how to play baseball and not to go crazy. While I think they understood the point, it didn't necessarily change their behavior. I often ended up having to tell several of them that if they wanted to see how the game turned out they would have to zip their lip and get back in their cage. Some failed to understand and got to go home early.

While I could hold sway over the coaches, the fans were another story. Oh, my goodness. I definitely did not remember people acting like that when I had played Little League. I once had a parent yell to a kid on the field that if the base runner tried to steal second, he needed to knock him down. Experience quickly taught me if you allowed too much of that type of talk it would quickly get out of control. I stopped the game and headed toward the stands. This encounter with the parent turned out to be one of my favorite Little League memories.

When I had called time-out and headed toward the stands, I noticed a county deputy had also began to move our way. I confronted the parent and told him I didn't need him yelling for one kid to knock another one down. He belligerently said he didn't mean it literally, and I asked if he thought a ten-year-old understood that. I guess in an effort to save face, the very large fellow stepped to the fence and engaged me in a staring contest. About that time the deputy stepped up beside the man. The fellow turned and looked at the deputy and belligerently asked him, "What are you going to do?"

The deputy did not miss a beat when he pointed at me and replied, "Whatever he tells me to."

The only thing bigger than the smile on my face was the frown on the fan's face. The guy looked at me and I told him to have a seat and we continued the game.

During the tournament, I had a fellow who evidently decided I could not hear his heckling from the stands well enough, so he took up a position against the fence almost directly behind me. It didn't matter whether or not the pitch was in the dirt or over the batter's head, according to him I missed the call.

I normally didn't put up with much heckling; however, I had come to understand that several of these folks obviously were allowed to get by with this type of behavior at their home field, so I tried to give them a little more leeway. A little, but not that much. It didn't take long until I had heard enough from the heckler, and I stopped the game and went over to tell him to knock it off. He quickly informed me he was just a fan, not a coach or manager, and I had no authority over him. Although that wasn't true, I didn't bother to explain how I could have him removed from the premises. I did tell him that if he continued ranting and raving I would clear the field of all players and explain to the hundreds of other fans that there would not be another pitch until he left the area. I let that sink in for a minute and then gave him the patented line, "If you want to see how this turns out, zip your lip." I returned to behind the plate and we finished the game.

After the game, I left the field and headed to the concession stand for a much-needed bottle of water. As I walked up I spotted the "fire guy" from the public launch incident years earlier. As is always the case with previous arrestees, you're never really sure how things will go. The man walked over to me and said, "Mr. Glover, don't you worry about that guy down there at the fence (my heckler). I've got my eye on him, and if he tries anything, he's gonna look like sausage going through a grinder when I push him through that chain-link fence!" I must admit that wasn't what I had anticipated, but I sure did appreciate it.

What that said to me was something I have tried to teach young officers for many years. How you treat people matters. While I wrote this guy a ticket, I did not try to embarrass him or show him up in front of his friends, and while he didn't appreciate the ticket, he obviously appreciated the way it was handled. It seems to me there is a rule about that kind of thing. It says do unto others as you would have them do unto you. It's a good rule to live by.

Start Praying

FOR THE FIRST SEVENTEEN YEARS of my career I worked a management area hunt somewhere in central Alabama every weekend of the gun deer season. In the late 1990s the Lowndes WMA was added to our district. Around this time a new wildlife biologist with a long last name was hired to work the WMA. Chris Jaworowski was fresh out of Auburn University. He was willing to work and willing to learn, so I enjoyed working with him. He would come and assist on my hunts, and we would always work deep into the night. He enjoyed doing enforcement work like I did and became quite good at it.

One sunny and cool winter day we were working a hunt on the Lowndes WMA, checking hunters as we came to them. We stopped a pickup, and Chris asked the driver for his WMA permit. Seeing a rifle in the passenger seat, Chris asked if the gun was unloaded. The man replied it was loaded. All WMAs had a universal regulation of no loaded firearms in a vehicle. Unfortunately, this was not a law outside of the WMA, and therefore it was a regularly violated rule. As Chris began explaining the law to the man I went around and retrieved the weapon and unloaded it. WMA regulations allowed us full search of any vehicle on the WMA. Our probable cause was the fact the vehicle was within the WMA boundaries. The law stated we could search the vehicles and persons for anything illegal. This could be the presence of a .22 cartridge, which basically allowed us to search everywhere. I raised the seat in the suspect's pickup and there found another rifle and a shotgun. I asked the man if the weapons were loaded and he said they were. Chris asked the man if he had any other weapons, and he replied he did. A look in his toolbox turned up four more weapons! In a somewhat bewildered tone Chris asked the man if he normally carried this arsenal around with him, and he indicated he did. Chris informed the man he was in violation of several WMA regulations. The man answered by saying he didn't need to get into trouble since he was a Baptist preacher. Chris didn't skip a beat when he replied, "You better start praying."

The preacher pointed to a vehicle that had pulled up behind his and told us the driver was his minister of music and the passenger was a deacon in his church. Chris asked for the preacher's driver's license, which was standard procedure when you were going to write someone a ticket. Unfortunately, when the man handed over the license, Chris just groaned. I had an idea what that groan meant, and I was correct: the man was a nonresident. Arresting a nonresident was a pain for us. Since we could not extradite for a misdemeanor, there was little incentive for a nonresident to return and answer a charge. Therefore, we did not allow nonresidents to sign a bond and be on their way; we normally took them to jail. In the event we arrested someone during a weekday, we could possibly get in touch with the judge, who could set their fine and allow them to come in and pay it and be on their way. Unfortunately, most of our cases were made on the weekend or in the evening, when judges were hard to track down. The violators could post a cash bond, and in the event they did not return for court their bond would be forfeited and used to pay their fine.

Chris and I conferred and decided that although he had several violations, we would write the man one ticket. Fortunately for the preacher, it was late on Friday afternoon and the judge was available to set a fine and allow the defendant to come in and pay it. Although he didn't ask, I volunteered he would probably have a good story for a sermon in the next few weeks. He said he would rather that no one found out about it. I looked around at the part of the congregation he had with him, and, having been a member of a Baptist church all my life, I thought, "Yeah like that's going to happen!"

In a way this story very much depicts the way we often view prayer. That is, we begin praying after something happens. While we should pray after unforeseen things occur, prayer should not be limited to an after-the-fact thought. The Bible says we should pray without ceasing. It tells us we should approach everything with prayer. The Lord knows everything. We don't pray to inform Him; we pray to acknowledge who He is and to invite Him into our life. Nothing keeps us from approaching God in prayer except our own choices.

Sadly, as I make this final edit to this story, it has been three days since my friend Chris was laid to rest—a young man of only forty-five, taken by complications from cancer surgery.

The Lowndes WMA was overrun with wild hogs. In part due to necessity and partially through his ambition, Chris became our departmental expert on the subject of wild pigs. Unfortunately, it is difficult to call dealing with wild pigs either management or eradication since you really can't eradicate them, and saying you are managing them is also a stretch. Suffice it to say Chris killed literally thousands of pigs and became well known as an authority on trapping and killing the pests. While wild pigs were a mere headache for some, they were devastating to many farmers. Chris worked closely with other agencies, including the Alabama Extension System and the USDA Wildlife Services groups on multiple projects and publications to assist landowners experiencing pig problems. Chris's expertise in this area unfortunately caused him several problems with the leadership of our department. It seemed that anytime a member of our staff excelled in any one area, our leadership would basically beat them over the head with their success. It was a sad phenomenon that was difficult to cope with. Eventually Chris left our agency and was hired by extension as a regional wildlife agent. There he was rightly regarded as an expert in his field.

Although he was no longer involved with our agency or law enforcement, his family requested that our departmental honor guard serve at his funeral. The request was granted. The twenty-one-gun salute and the presentation of the flag to his wife by the honor guard was a fitting farewell for one who had served the citizens of our state as a wildlife biologist and CEO for eighteen years. At the conclusion of the service I stood with the many other officers reminiscing. My good friend Lt. Michael East said to me, "This just shows we never know if we will see tomorrow," and I replied, "Yes, but fortunately we can take care of our eternal future today."

During the graveside service the priest had stated that Chris would rest here until the Lord came to get him on the day of His glorious return. In his southern drawl, Michael said to me, "I know what that fellow said, but when I go I will be with the Lord that day. They ain't gonna be no waiting around!"

I replied, "I'm with you, brother."

If you don't know for sure that when you die you will immediately be in heaven with the Savior, today is the day to ensure that. As Chris's untimely death once again proved, tomorrow isn't guaranteed. Rest in peace my good friend. Until we meet again.

It's Who You Know

WORKING AN AREA that has been illegally baited to attract wildlife is normally not nearly as easy as it may seem. There are several factors involved. First you must locate the bait. Even after receiving good information, a baited area can still be like trying to find a needle in a haystack. Once you are fortunate enough to locate the baited site then you can begin to check the area for hunter activity. In some rare instances, this isn't a problem. Normally checking the bait isn't a problem; checking the bait without being seen—now that's often the challenge. For some reason, even people who call and report law violators will turn around and tell the people they have called the game warden. This is even also true with people who see the game warden drive by or park down the road and slip out of his truck. Not getting caught is often quite a feat.

Checking baited areas is often a very dangerous situation. This is especially true when the hunter does not have a shooting house or blind at the site. It is an eerie feeling to walk up on a baited area and then locate the hunter who has been watching you all the time with gun in hand. Unfortunately, some setups demand that you walk directly into the hunter's line of sight. Although we always wanted to approach from the back side, it wasn't always possible. Sometimes you didn't know which side was the back side.

It's Who You Know

Prior to the deer season, I received information concerning an area that was supposedly baited for deer. I made my way into the area and found it was indeed baited with corn in feeders in two fields. Each field had a shooting house, which the hunter would likely hunt from. Everything indicated it was a gun-hunting setup, so I waited until the opening day of gun season to check it. That check and several subsequent checks revealed no activity.

Upon returning from a brief trip home for Christmas, I decided to once again check the area. As I approached the trail leading to the baited field I came upon a four-wheeler. Obviously, this was a good sign. I slipped along the trail toward the field. This shooting house was different than most in that the entrance was located on the side that faced the field. I felt this would be in my favor. However, as I eased to within twenty yards of the house I realized my luck wasn't as good as I had hoped. As I looked past the house into the field, I noticed the feeder was gone.

The disappearance of the feeder presented a problem in that at this time our bait law stated the hunter must either know or should have known the bait was present. This was pretty easy to prove with a feeder full of corn in the field. However, without the feeder, even with corn on the ground, the hunter could claim he had not seen the bait, and I would be hard pressed to prove he had. All of this was going through my head as I stealthily approached the stand.

As I eased to within thirty feet of the house, I could see a hunter through the side window. He was facing the field. As I moved still closer, I noticed he appeared to be smoking. As I was now ten feet from the man, it was obvious from the smell he wasn't smoking tobacco. Just then the man turned and looked out the window and saw me standing there staring at him. He immediately began to move furtively. I stepped closer and told him to raise his hands over his head. This was always a dangerous time. In this situation, it would be almost impossible for the man to get a long gun out of the window and pointed in my direction; however, I have taken many people out of shooting houses who possessed handguns.

I moved closer to the house, and he raised his hands. He was holding a backpack. I moved around in front of the house and told him to slowly put the backpack on the floor. I again told him to raise his hands. I reached in the door of the house and took his rifle and his backpack and instructed him to exit the house. He slowly came out, and I realized he wasn't much more than a kid (actually twenty years old). However, a kid can kill you just like anyone else. That is especially true when you've just caught him smoking dope, and he doesn't know what the future may hold for him.

I asked if he had any weapons other than his rifle, and he said he did not. I patted him down to be sure. (I was lied to once—or was it a bunch of times?) I unloaded his rifle and opened the backpack, which contained some hunting paraphernalia, a marijuana pipe, a small bag of marijuana, and a can of beer. I asked how old he was, and he replied he was twenty. I informed him he was under arrest.

Leaving his rifle and backpack on the ground, I told him to follow me. We walked across the field to where the feeder had been earlier. As I suspected there was some corn on the ground; however, seeing how it was in the grass one hundred yards from the shooting house, I knew I would be hard pressed to make that case.

We walked back to the stand. I retrieved the evidence, and we headed toward the next field. En route I asked the young man if someone was in the next field, and he said he thought so. As we neared the field I spotted a young man in the shooting house overlooking the food plot.

The hunter saw us approaching and began to gather his belongings. I instructed him to unload his rifle and come down. He also had a backpack, which I searched but failed to find anything illegal. Thinking he probably threw anything illegal out of the house when he saw me coming, I thoroughly searched the area but found nothing. The feeder had been removed from this field as well. However, the subject did not have a hunting license. I issued him a citation for the offense and explained his friend was under arrest and I would be taking him to the Coosa County jail in Rockford.

As we rode to the jail I learned the defendant was a junior at the University of Alabama with plans to become an attorney. He was a very articulate and polished individual. I explained what his charges would be and he would likely have a $1,000 bond. I was quite taken aback when he replied, "I've got that much." I wondered to myself, what twenty-year-old kid sits in a shooting house with a thousand dollars in his pocket?

We got to the jail, and I took him inside and started the paperwork. He was allowed to make a phone call and started the booking procedure with the jailer. The kid was very nice, well mannered, and no trouble whatsoever.

I had finished the paperwork and was in the lobby of the jail when a fellow showed up and said he was there to bond the defendant out. The man introduced himself to me as Ben Griffin and asked if I was the arresting officer. I told him I was. He asked me what the charges were, and I explained the boy was charged with second-degree possession of marijuana and possession of drug paraphernalia. I told him I did not charge him with a minor in possession of alcohol or hunting by the aid of bait, although that was my probable cause for being there.

Mr. Griffin asked if I would consider charging the subject with hunting over bait and dropping the other charges.

I told him no, the young man had already been charged and placed in jail.

At this point the man decided to try a different tactic. It was one I was very familiar with. He handed me his business card and stated he owned several businesses and had over seven hundred people working for him. I felt I knew where this was headed, and I replied that with those assets I didn't figure he would have any problem coming up with the $1,000 bond. This took him aback a little, but he quickly shot back he knew the commissioner of the department of conservation well and had done business with him several times. When that didn't get a response, he used a line I always find amusing when it comes from folks under arrest or those associated with them: "We always do our best to follow the game laws." Seeing he wasn't getting anywhere fast I guess he felt it was time to play his trump card. He said, "You should know I'm close personal friends with the governor."

At this point, I had had enough, and I looked Mr. Griffin right in the eye and told him there was no one he could name who could undo what had been done today. Nobody was going to make this situation go away, and the best thing he could do was to bond the boy out and hire him a good attorney and be in court. With that I showed him who he needed to talk to, and I left the jail.

The badge is a great equalizer versus wealth. Although someone's wealth and status may very well help them out in the long run, while you are out there one on one, the ability to take them to jail trumps almost every card that can be played.

The court date rolled around, and the young man showed up in a fine suit and with a high-dollar attorney. As a matter of fact, he had two attorneys. The lead attorney told me he had spoken with the judge and thought we would be able to work out an agreement. It wasn't a good sign when the judge summoned me and said he wanted to handle the cases in his office. I knew he wasn't handling things behind closed doors because he wanted to throw the book at the young man. As the defendant, his attorneys and I stood before his desk; the judge informed me he had worked out an agreement in these cases. He did not ask for my blessing or even a comment, and I knew better than to offer one. He said the young man would pay a $500 fine and court costs in each case. He would be placed on one year of probation, during which time he would submit to drug testing every month. In the event all of his tests were clean for one year the charges would be removed from his record. The judge looked at me with the look that said, "You will agree to this," and I nodded my head in agreement. I turned to the defendant and told him I felt he had the opportunity for a great future, and I thought this incident would help him toward that. He thanked me, and I left the office.

Now that's a long story to get to the message I have for you. The message is actually based on Mr. Griffin and others like him. Mr. Griffin thought because he was a wealthy man he should have special privilege. He felt because he normally followed the law he should receive a break. In addition, he thought because of his wealth and because of whom he knew he deserved special treatment.

Some people, actually many people, believe it's who you know that makes all the difference. They are so right, but not in the way they think. The Bible says he that does wrong shall receive for the wrong he has done AND there is no respect of persons. While I am far from a Bible scholar, I believe God added the ending to that verse just for folks who think the law doesn't apply to them.

We all are in need of forgiveness. Romans says all have sinned and come short of the glory of God. Salvation isn't anything we can merit. It isn't anything that can be bought. The Lord reminds us our righteousness is like filthy rags. However, the joyous irony is while we were yet sinners, Christ died for us.

Just like I told the millionaire in this story, what has happened cannot be undone. Sin has consequences. However, thank God, there is such thing as forgiveness. Jesus stands ready to forgive us today. If you want to know somebody who can *really* help you, know Jesus!

Divine Appointment

"SIR, IS THERE SOME REASON why you were going over one hundred miles per hour today?"

The man wearing leather and Vietnam veteran insignia replied, "I was just being stupid." I couldn't argue with that.

While I can't speak for all law enforcement officers and it may be different elsewhere, myself and most of the other rural law enforcement officers I have been acquainted with were law enforcement officers 24/7. As a wildlife biologist, law enforcement wasn't my primary duty assignment; however, I learned early on you don't just take off your law enforcement hat. I feel officers who take their job seriously understand you can't break the law today and enforce it tomorrow. Law enforcement is very much a way of life. The officer looks at things differently than most people, doesn't trust easily, and is skeptical about most things and people. It can be a stressful way of life. Actually, it is a stressful way of life. Although officers attempt to live by the book, they are human and do make mistakes. While some feel their position puts them above the law, most realize they have a responsibility to practice what they preach or enforce.

After a long day of working as a wildlife biologist, which had unfortunately transformed into a lot of looking at the computer monitor in my office, I was headed home. It was a beautiful, crisp winter day, the twenty-ninth of December.

As I traveled west on Highway 22 I could not help but notice how stunning the clear blue sky was. As I glanced at my rearview mirror I noticed a motorcycle passing several cars behind me. Although we were approaching a hill, it was obvious the rider wasn't backing off, and he was moving. Just as the bike passed me, a voice came over my radio and asked, "Are you going to stop him?" I immediately looked in my mirror for the car I was sure was pursuing the speeding driver, but did not see one.

Seeing how the biker was traveling at a high rate of speed and had passed me in a no-passing zone I activated my lights and siren and began pursuing the subject. I answered the deputy who had called and asked where he was. He replied he was in the yard at his house I had just passed and added the chief deputy was coming to assist me. I called the Coosa County SO and reported to the dispatcher I was attempting to catch up with a red motorcycle westbound on Highway 22 in the Hissop community.

I was quickly in excess of 100 miles per hour and did not appear to be gaining on the suspect. Motorcycle chases were tough. The machines could easily reach high speed and could easily out maneuver my SUV. Working with the SO I once chased a motorcycle thirty-five miles and at speeds of 126 miles per hour! That's another story!

Just as I began to consider breaking off the pursuit, I noticed the vehicle was slowing in preparation to turn into the Indian Hills Motorcycle Resort. I thought that's just what I need: to chase an outlaw motorcyclist into our rural equivalent of a biker bar. However, I dutifully followed the violator. Fortunately, the fellow pulled over about one hundred yards into the resort before we made it to the watering hole, which, I found out later, held approximately thirty beer drinkers. I exited my vehicle and asked for his driver's license. He handed it to me, and I asked, "Is there some reason you are running over one hundred miles per hour today?" to which he replied, "I was just being stupid."

As I returned to my vehicle, Coosa County Chief Deputy Ken Whitehead pulled in behind me, followed immediately by Rockford Police Chief Mike Arms. Although everything was under control, I was glad to see them. I quickly told them what had occurred, and I ran the driver's license through the SO. It came back as current and with no warrants. I began the process—or ordeal—of writing the man a couple of traffic tickets.

Although we, as state police officers, had full powers of arrest and could write traffic tickets, it was not common for us to do so. Unlike my game and fish bond book that stayed in my pocket or on my dash, my uniform traffic citation (UTC) book took some digging to uncover. Once I found it and dusted it off, I had to find an old ticket to use as an example for writing the new one. A quick look revealed it had been four years since I had written a UTC! However, it was sort of like riding a bicycle, and I was soon well into completing the first citation.

While writing I noticed another vehicle as it pulled in behind our vehicles and watched as the occupant got out and headed in our direction. The man spoke with the deputy and, noticing me, asked, "What's the game warden doing in here?"

I looked at the man and said, "When they can't catch 'em, they call us."

The look on the guy's face was priceless. (I later learned he was the owner of the resort.) Although my vehicle had more blue lights flashing than the two police cruisers on the scene combined, some folks still did not consider us police officers, and they definitely didn't expect us to make a traffic stop.

I finished writing tickets for speeding one hundred plus and illegal passing and had the man sign them. I told him I would see him in court in Rockford on January 17. As soon as I informed him of the court date a look of panic came across the man's face. He told me he had a conflict with that date and asked if I could possibly change it. He had been nice enough, and I agreed to set it for the February court date. He thanked me and again apologized for acting stupid. I told him everyone acts stupid every once in a while, but doing it on a motorcycle at over one hundred miles per hour is a good way to dull your axe! Noticing his jacket was covered with Vietnam veteran insignia, I asked if he had been in-country, and he stated he had. I told him I appreciated his service to our country. He thanked me, and we went our separate ways.

I anticipated the man would probably take it tough in court since our judge frowned on people going in excess of one hundred miles per hour. However, the judge did have an affinity for motorcycles, so I wasn't sure how it would turn out. There were often many facets to any court case.

The February court date rolled around with district criminal court commencing at 9:00 a.m. As a general rule, wildlife cases dominated the docket during the winter months. I endured a nice sparring match with a defense attorney and the ADA concerning some game and fish violations; however, we prevailed, and the defendants were convicted. Court was adjourned around noon. District traffic court began at 1:00 p.m. Although we were a small rural county our court handled a high volume of cases. There were 361 traffic cases on the docket, which meant a long afternoon was in store. Although the docket was long, there were only about fifty people in the courtroom. This was not unusual. Folks with traffic offenses were often given the opportunity to send in their fine and costs. Therefore, many of them would opt not to appear before the judge. Unfortunately, several of them would end up "forgetting" to take care of their tickets and would end up with their license suspended and warrants for their arrest.

As I scanned the folks in the court room I was surprised to see my biker was not present. I was assuming I would recognize the man, although I had been wrong about that before. It is amazing how different people can look in the courtroom compared to when you encounter them on the road. A suit and a haircut can bring about an incredible transformation!

I monitored the docket as the judge waded through the numerous bench trials until my case was called. When the defendant did not appear, the judge issued a failure-to-appear warrant in each case, and I was free to leave.

Days later, the judge signed the warrants and suspended the man's driver's license. The clerk told me the warrants were "no bond," meaning when the defendant was arrested he would be held in jail until the next court date. This was unfortunate since the man had a good job, had been cordial and respectful, and this would no doubt be a big hassle if not worse. Of course, he was the one who had failed to show up and had set the consequences in motion.

With the next court date fast approaching, I decided to try to contact the man and advise I had warrants for him and it would be in his best interest to be in court on the next court date. I phoned the number on the ticket and reached a recording telling me the number was no longer in service.

Until this point I had not felt the man had been deceptive with me; however, someone having their phone disconnected made one wonder.

After over two thousand arrests and thousands more encounters, I felt I was a pretty good judge of character, and I had not read this guy as the type who would not take care of an obligation. However, due to his having not shown up for court and having provided a possibly bogus phone number I was beginning to question whether or not I might have read him wrong.

I decided I would attempt to locate the fellow in the white pages on the internet, so I entered his name on the search line. Although no phone number or address came up, something else did. It was a notice posted on the Patriot Guard Riders website. It stated another armed forces hero had been lost when Bobby "Red Dog" Roberts was killed in a motorcycle accident on a rural Alabama road.

Although the name matched the subject I had ticketed, I knew I would need to verify things. I phoned the office he had told me he worked in and asked the lady who answered if I could speak with Mr. Roberts. She initially placed me on hold and then returned to the phone and said she was sorry to have to tell me, but Mr. Roberts had been killed in a motorcycle accident. I told her what my interest was and thanked her for the confirmation. I contacted the court and told them they could recall the warrants and dismiss the cases.

This was an interesting turn of events. I must admit my first thought was to wonder if Mr. Roberts's fast driving had been the cause of the accident that claimed his life. I had no way of knowing; however, I knew his driving behavior on the day of our encounter could likely have led to his death. As a matter of fact, I had told him that and urged him to be more careful.

When I handed Mr. Roberts those tickets, I dare say it never crossed his mind he might not be able to keep the appointment. He was sadly mistaken. He didn't know another appointment, a divine appointment, had already been scheduled. This appointment is one we will all have! No man knows the day or hour when Christ will return or when he will go to meet Him. But rest assured we will.

I am reminded of the man in Luke who made plans for what he would do with his riches, and the Lord said to him, "You fool, this very night your life will be demanded from you."

We all believe that will not happen to us, don't we? Proverbs 27:1 says, "Do not boast about tomorrow, for you do not know what a day may bring."

The Bible is chock full of advice. It says don't be caught sleeping. The end is near; be alert and pray. Are you ready?

You may be running from God at one hundred miles per hour, but he can stop you on a dime. Although Jesus holds the keys to heaven and hell, He gives us the choice as to where we will spend eternity. It's a decision we all make one way or the other.

Choose wisely.

God bless.

www.ingramcontent.com/pod-product-compliance
Lightning Source LLC
Chambersburg PA
CBHW050630300426
44112CB00012B/1735